The World of
Dürer

TIME LIFE BOOKS ®

The World of Dürer

1471-1528

by Francis Russell
and
the Editors of TIME-LIFE BOOKS

Time Incorporated, New York

TIME-LIFE BOOKS

FOUNDER: Henry R. Luce 1898-1967

Editor-in-Chief: Hedley Donovan
Chairman of the Board: Andrew Heiskell
President: James R. Shepley

Vice Chairman: Roy E. Larsen

MANAGING EDITOR: Jerry Korn
Assistant Managing Editors: Ezra Bowen,
David Maness, Martin Mann, A. B. C. Whipple
Planning Director: Oliver E. Allen
Art Director: Sheldon Cotler
Chief of Research: Beatrice T. Dobie
Director of Photography: Melvin L. Scott
Senior Text Editors: Diana Hirsh, William Frankel
Assistant Planning Director: Carlotta Kerwin
Assistant Art Director: Arnold C. Holeywell
Assistant Chief of Research: Myra Mangan

PUBLISHER: Joan D. Manley
General Manager: John D. McSweeney
Business Manager: Nicholas J. C. Ingleton
Sales Director: Carl G. Jaeger
Promotion Director: Paul R. Stewart
Public Relations Director: Nicholas Benton

TIME-LIFE LIBRARY OF ART
Editorial Staff for *The World of Dürer:*
EDITOR: Robert Morton
Associate Editor: Diana Hirsh
Text Editor: Harvey B. Loomis
Picture Editor: Jane Scholl
Designer: Paul Jensen
Assistant Designer: Leonard Wolfe
Staff Writer: Frank Kendig
Chief Researcher: Martha T. Goolrick
Researchers: Susan Grafman, Judith Levenson,
James MaHood, Rosemary O'Connell, Jenifer Ratliff,
Susanna Seymour, Yvonne Wong
Art Assistant: Nancy Earle

EDITORIAL PRODUCTION
Production Editor: Douglas B. Graham
Assistant Production Editors:
Gennaro C. Esposito, Feliciano Madrid
Quality Director: Robert L. Young
Assistant Quality Director: James J. Cox
Associate: Serafino J. Cambareri
Copy Staff: Eleanore W. Karsten (chief), Muriel Clarke,
Florence Keith, Pearl Sverdlin
Picture Department: Dolores A. Littles, Joan Lynch
Traffic: Carmen McLellan

About the Author

Francis Russell, historian and literary critic, has written for American, Canadian, Irish and English magazines. His books include *Three Studies in 20th Century Obscurity*, a trio of critical essays on James Joyce, Franz Kafka and Gertrude Stein; *The Great Interlude: Neglected Events and Persons from the First World War to the Depression*; and *Tragedy in Dedham: The Story of the Sacco-Vanzetti Case*, which received an "Edgar" from the Mystery Writers of America as the best fact-crime book of 1962. Mr. Russell's interest in Dürer began during his student years at a German university.

The Consulting Editor

H. W. Janson is Professor of Fine Arts at New York University, where he is also Chairman of the Department of Fine Arts at Washington Square College. Among his numerous publications are his *History of Art* and *The Sculpture of Donatello*.

The Consultant for This Book

Ruth Saunders Magurn is a former Curator of Prints at Harvard University's Fogg Art Museum, where she studied Dürer's works intensively. She is also the translator and editor of *The Letters of Peter Paul Rubens*, a result of her special interest in the 17th Century.

On the Slipcase

A self-portrait shows Dürer proud and self-assured at the age of 27, wearing a fashionable cap. The entire painting is on page 178.

End Papers

Front: Dürer produced these fanciful pen-and-ink sketches of animals, human forms and mythological creatures on his first journey to Italy.
Back: These drawings, also in pen and ink, were made by Dürer in the Netherlands, and include studies of lions and other animals sketched from life, in a zoo.

The following departments and individuals of Time Inc. helped to produce this book: Editorial Production, Norman Airey; Library, Benjamin Lightman; Picture Collection, Doris O'Neil; Photographic Laboratory, George Karas; TIME-LIFE News Service, Murray J. Gart; Correspondents Maria Vincenza Aloisi and Joan Dupont (Paris), Friso Endt (Amsterdam), Elisabeth Kraemer and Lexi Blomever (Bonn), Traudl Lessing (Vienna), Barbara Moir and Margot Hapgood (London), Ann Natanson (Rome), Alex de Fontaines (Geneva).

Contents

6

I

An Art
for Everyman

The piece of turf must have been dug not long after sunrise, for the florets of the dandelions are tightly closed, and the leaves below them are still moist with the morning coolness. Such a clump of plants and grasses might be found today along any country road, in Europe or America, where it dips down into the dampness of a hollow. Besides the dandelions there are the fleshy leaves of the great plantain, creeping Charlie, and a dwarfed feathery shoot of yarrow. As for the grasses, they are of the most commonplace—meadow grass, cock's foot, the thin spikes of heath rush.

Yet common as they are, each plant, each closed blossom, each grassblade, stands by itself in its moment of summer, abstracted from time. Its livingness is as apparent as it was on that morning in 1503 when Albrecht Dürer dug this clump of earth to carry home and place at eye level so he could capture it in a watercolor sketch.

Painting *The Great Piece of Turf (page 32)* was an exercise for Dürer, a welcome change of pace in the production of more ambitious works. Yet this simple study and a handful of other pictures have fixed his art more firmly in public esteem than all the rest of his prodigious output. Doubtless Dürer would have been pleased at this perpetuation of a summer morning's expedition. "For in truth," as he wrote, "art is implicit in nature, and whoever can extract it has it."

He had sensed the force of his talents early, judging from the poised assurance of the extraordinary self-portrait that he drew at the age of 13 *(opposite)*. Yet life had not intended him for an artist and scarcely intended him for a German. His father, a master goldsmith, was a native of Hungary who had wandered westward and settled in the free city of Nuremberg. Here Albrecht was born, in 1471, and after a few years of schooling took his place as apprentice in his father's workshop, as was expected in such hereditary crafts. But he grew restive, and soon confessed that he wanted to be a painter. Although it was almost unheard of for an apprentice to change his occupation, the elder Dürer recognized his son's unique ability and allowed him to set aside his goldsmith's tools. With parental blessing, the boy entered

When he was only 13 Albrecht Dürer gazed into a mirror and produced this amazingly accomplished self-portrait. Executed in the exacting silverpoint medium—a technique that employs a silver stylus and specially coated paper, and permits no erasures—this drawing is both his earliest known work and the first recognized self-portrait in German art.

Self-Portrait at 13, 1484

the workshop of the Nuremberg painter Michael Wolgemut, mixing pigments and doing all the other chores required of a novice.

Through this turn of events began the career of Germany's greatest artist. When fame came to him, some time around 1500, it came swiftly and unstintingly. His name and his works were celebrated not only throughout his own country—hitherto more accustomed to painters of merely local or provincial renown—but all across Europe. Dürer was a true artist of the masses; thanks to the recent perfection of the printing press, his woodcuts and engravings could be reproduced and circulated on a wide scale. For the price of pennies, a Dürer woodcut could hang even in the home of the humble. At the same time, because of his command of the humanistic learning of his day, he knew how to appeal to the most refined tastes as well.

A supreme master of the graphic arts, Dürer was no less gifted as a painter, whether of landscapes, portraits or religious subjects. Whatever his medium or theme, the fundamental components he brought to his art were the same. He had both a strong faith and a rational mind, so that his intensity of expression was matched by his clarity of purpose. He had an analytical eye as accurate in its observations of the material world as that of his Italian contemporary, Leonardo da Vinci. There were, indeed, striking parallels between the two men. Both were consummate draftsmen. Both wrote and thought and felt deeply about their art. Personally, both tended to be reserved, indifferent to women, and vain to the point almost of narcissism, as was evidenced by an interest in fine clothes and, in Dürer, by a penchant for self-portraits.

Added to Dürer's qualities of mind and eye was an extraordinary facility of hand, fully responsive to his dictates, equally adept with the paintbrush or the burin, the steel tool required in delicate copper engravings. After his death his fellow Nuremberger Joachim Camerarius, a professor who published a Latin translation of two of Dürer's books on the subject of human proportions, prefaced the text with a memoir of his good friend. He wrote of Dürer's intelligent head, his flashing eyes, his nobly formed nose, his broad chest, then noted: "But his fingers—you would vow you had never seen anything more elegant."

Camerarius continued: "What shall I say of the steadiness and exactitude of his hand? You might swear that rule, square or compasses had been employed to draw lines which he, in fact, drew with the brush, or very often with pencil or pen. . . . I see I shall not be believed by my readers when I relate that sometimes he would draw separately . . . the different parts of bodies which, when joined together, agreed with one another so well that nothing could have fitted better. In fact, this consummate artist's mind, endowed with all knowledge and understanding of the truth . . . governed and guided his hand and bade it trust to itself without any other aids. . . . And this was a subject of greatest wonder to most distinguished painters who, from their own great experience, could understand the difficulty of the thing."

Dürer grew up in that singular period of tension when the Middle Ages were on the wane, overborne by the Renaissance from the South and the coming Reformation in the North. He was a man of his time and yet in advance of it, aware of its perils but also of its potentialities. This awareness underlay his art and helped make it great.

The artistic tradition into which he was born was still largely medieval. Men of superb talents pursued it, but in a land as physically divided as 15th Century Germany they were rarely known beyond their own home grounds. Local schools of art flourished along the Rhine and the Danube and the Baltic Coast, in Bavaria and Franconia and Bohemia. Styles of painting varied but generally fell into two broad categories: a "soft" style, marked by grace and charm and ornateness, and later a "hard" style, sometimes severely simple and sometimes infinitely complex in composition, but in either case with figures of a pronounced sculptural quality. Stephan Lochner of Cologne epitomized the soft style with his idyllic Madonnas *(page 43)*. The hard style produced such masterpieces as the stark and powerful *Christ Walking on the Water (page 44)* by Conrad Witz of Basel, and the intricately carved and painted *Altarpiece of the Four Latin Fathers (page 45)* by the Tyrolean sculptor-painter Michael Pacher.

Whatever the separate styles of Dürer's predecessors, their art reflected a curious blend of the mystic and the material. Gothic expressiveness—gentle or brooding or frenzied—shared room in their works with realistic detail. Yet in an age of faith, however racked by doubt, there could be no question as to the religious context in which these men labored. Lochner could paint flowers and animals, but he painted them in settings for the Virgin. Witz depicted a recognizable landscape of the shores of Lake Geneva, but he made it a backdrop for Christ on the Sea of Galilee. Neither painter would have been so bold as to paint a piece of turf alone. Dürer did so unhesitatingly. In his eyes each sprouting plant, each blade of grass, contained its own religious essence.

Opening the Gothic windows of German art was one of Dürer's great contributions to his age. Another was his special awareness of the enormous ramifications of the revolution wrought by the printing press. It was easy enough to foresee that words in print would transform the minds of more men than ever before; it was less easy to perceive that images in print could transform men's esthetic tastes. The woodcuts that followed immediately on the invention of printing had been simple affairs; Dürer elevated them into high works of art. The great humanist teacher Erasmus of Rotterdam, marveling at the black-and-white enchantment of Dürer's prints, wrote: "He observes accurately proportions and harmonies. Nay he even depicts that which cannot be depicted: fire, rays of light, thunder . . . lightning . . . all the sensations and emotions; in sum, the whole mind of man as it reflects itself in the behavior of the body, and almost the voice itself."

Had he never stirred from Nuremberg, Dürer would have expanded the horizons of German art. But he was destined to serve it most notably by a visit beyond his country's borders. Many outside influences—Flemish, French, Burgundian, Italian—had filtered in to challenge German parochialism. Dürer, however, went forth to see for himself, journeying to Italy on a mission of artistic exploration that was later to become standard practice for painters of every nationality. Out of this

One of the earliest book illustrations ever printed, this woodcut depicts the grinning figure of Death presiding over a dead woman and her bereaved family. It appeared in 1463 in a popular allegory, *Der Ackermann aus Böhmen,* published by the first printer of illustrated books, Albrecht Pfister of Bamberg. The spare, outline design, deliberately kept simple to facilitate hand-coloring of the print, is also partly a reflection of the primitive state of the woodcutting art at the time.

adventure he achieved, virtually singlehanded, one of the most momentous fusions in history. He united the energy of the late Gothic with the form of the Renaissance, the somber exactness of the North with the sunny classical exuberance of the South, and thereby opened the way to a truly European art.

Any artist is of course a child of his time, from the fashioner of the Sphinx working within the stylistic rigidities of the Egyptian dynastic tradition to a Picasso devising innovations for himself. The universal artist carries over beyond his age. The Sphinx had meaning for Napoleon, and for us; perhaps Picasso's *Guernica* will have meaning for another generation—and perhaps not. For when men respond to a work of art of another era, not knowing why themselves, they are moved by something akin to the Platonic idea. The sculpture, the temple, the picture, the drawing of a simple piece of turf, attain a kind of elemental immortality, at least as measured by our ephemeral time scale.

Viewing Dürer's work through 20th Century eyes, with the 16th Century theological aspects long since removed, we value him for other qualities than did his contemporaries. What was important to them often seems of dubious significance to us. What we find most significant, they might not have understood. Yet throughout his work the sense of timelessness remains.

Dürer has suffered as well as benefited from the almost unlimited possibilities of cheap modern reproduction. His small watercolors of plants and animals appear on postcards in cut-rate art shops next to Utrillo views of Montmartre. During the National Socialist period in Germany he was extolled as the first of the "true German" artists, and there was scarcely a boy or girl belonging to the Hitler Youth who did not have on the bedroom wall a framed copy of Dürer's watercolor of the crouching hare or the bunch of violets.

The most often reproduced, the most widely familiar of Dürer's works is the gray and white brush drawing on blue-grounded paper of the *Hands of an Apostle,* known generally—and by many who are not even aware of the artist's name—as "The Praying Hands." Commerce has made the most of those hands. They have appeared not only on innumerable postcards but occasionally on cigarette boxes, and even recently in the third dimension as plastic book ends.

The actual drawing of the *Hands* is one of a score of studies of individual figures, heads, hands, feet and draperies that Dürer sketched in 1508 in preparation for an altarpiece, *The Assumption and Coronation of the Virgin,* commissioned by the Frankfort merchant Jacob Heller for the Dominican Church of St. Thomas in that city. For 13 months Dürer worked on the painting, determined to make it so sound and beautiful "that it will remain bright and fresh for five hundred years."

Unfortunately for his intentions, the central panel of the Heller altarpiece was sold a century later by the Dominicans to Duke Maximilian of Bavaria, and in 1729 it was destroyed by a fire. Only a copy has survived, along with the preliminary sketches that Dürer customarily fitted together for his final pictures almost like pieces in a jigsaw puzzle. It has sometimes been said that the sketch of the hands was modeled after those of the painter's mother. In fact, the hands may be his own. In those basic tools of his trade he was able to sense the durable beyond himself. Above a network of veins the ascetic, somewhat gnarled fingers come to a point like a Gothic arch. There is the same limitless quality, the striving to break through spatial and temporal boundaries, that is the unique mark of the Gothic. Here the hands of the Apostle in prayer have become the hands of Faust, seeking to encompass all knowledge.

Almost as well known as the *Hands* is Dürer's "The Four Horsemen" of *The Apocalypse (page 101).* Indeed our enduring conception of the Four Horsemen has been formed less by the sixth chapter of the Revelation of St. John than by Dürer's woodcut. It is through his concentrated line that we visualize the brief verses from John's account of the vision of the future that he experienced in his imprisonment on the isle of Patmos. The image-haunted saint saw four mounted figures against a dissolving sky: the crowned rider with his bow on a white horse; the rider with a great sword on a red horse; the rider with a pair of balances in his hand, on a black horse; Death on a pale horse. John named only Death among the four. Dürer took this imagery and translated it into a picture after his own more precise vision. His four galloping figures on fearsome horses, actualized as temporal beings, have become universal symbols: Conquest; War; Pestilence, swinging the scales of famine; Death, with his mad relentless eyes, on his haggard steed. Ever since its appearance, Dürer's woodcut has seemed to mirror times of trouble, and the more global war has become, the more it has echoed the sweep of his horsemen across the skies.

Dürer's *Four Horsemen* was the most memorable of a series of 15 woodcuts illustrating the Book of Revelation that he published in 1498 after his return from Italy. He was 27 at the time, and had begun, after a number of experiments, to sign his pictures with the final form of the monogram that would become his trademark. The text of the Book of Revelation was printed on the reverse side of the woodcuts, which are approximately 15 inches high. Choosing the medium of the woodcut rather than the more sophisticated copper engraving, Dürer intended this work as a sermon for ordinary men and women—often illiterate— that would sustain them in the time of turbulence and foreboding in which they lived. Not only in form but in content, as the German critic Max Steck pointed out, the *Apocalypse* woodcuts summon the beholder to change his way of life.

Dürer's now famous "Praying Hands," a brush drawing on a blue-grounded paper, was intended simply as a preliminary study for an altarpiece commissioned by a wealthy Frankfort citizen, Jacob Heller. Nevertheless, the drawing is finished down to the last detail, because Dürer planned to transpose it exactly in the final oil painting.

A s overwhelming in its withdrawn way as the charging horsemen of the Apocalypse are in theirs is the engraving of the brooding female figure that Dürer made after his mother's lingering and painful death in 1514. Against a bat's flaring wings in the seascape background of the picture he drew the letters MELENCOLIA I. This picture *(page 115)* has had more interpreters and interpretations than almost any other work in the history of German art. Yet in a sense it is self-explanatory. The profound moods of depression that at times possess us all beyond reason are summarized in the full-bodied, heavy-winged woman with her great eyes staring into space. The infinite horizon of Dürer's melancholy bridges the years to the isolation of each of us now alive, to

 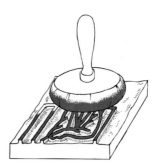

Making a Woodcut

A woodcut begins as a design sketched on a block of wood that has been covered with a white ground. All wood not part of the design is dug out with a sharp gouge.

The raised design is coated with ink by rocking a leather-covered wooden tool called a dabber over the block. The gouged areas are thus kept ink-free.

what the novelist Joseph Conrad called the loneliness of every human soul from the cradle to the grave.

Above the woman's garlanded head is a wall to which is attached a balance, an hourglass, a bell and a square of 16 numbers—four to a side, in which each column, whether added up horizontally or vertically, produces the figure 34. The woman holds a book in her lap and dividers in her hand; keys hang from the belt of her full skirt. Her purse rests at the edge of her skirt close to a sleeping dog. Scattered about at her feet are various carpenters' tools: a saw, a plane, a T-square, pincers, nails and an awl, and farther off a hammer and brazier. Then there are other apparently unrelated objects: a sphere, a granite polyhedron, a ladder, a small cherub perched on a millstone and writing in a book. In the seascape background a rainbow stretches across the sky, and a comet sends out its radiance, like the aurora borealis, over a distant promontory with gabled houses.

Baffling as it may be to us, the significance of the numerous objects and numbers in the *Melencolia I* was less of a puzzle to Dürer's contemporaries. They were as accustomed to similar allegories—in the stained glass and the stone portal figures of cathedrals, in altarpieces, statuary and carvings—as we are familiar with such political symbols as the donkey, the elephant, Uncle Sam, John Bull, the hammer and sickle, the swastika or the rising sun. Dürer himself gave the meaning of two of his symbols: "The keys mean power; the purse means wealth."

Long after the contemporary allusiveness was lost, the *Melencolia I* was scrutinized by a succession of scholars persuaded that somewhere in the picture there must be a hidden key to the understanding of the

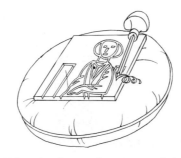 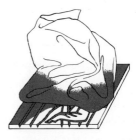

Making an Engraving

Using a sharply pointed instrument called a burin, the engraver incises his design into the surface of a metal plate, which is usually made of highly polished copper.

After any roughness on the edges of the grooves has been smoothed, ink is applied with a cloth, filling the grooves. The surface is wiped and the plate is ready to print.

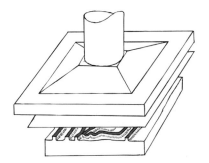

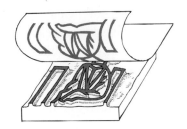

A sheet of paper is next placed on the inked block and imprinted on it by means of a vertical press. Pressure is applied gently so as to avoid damaging the wooden relief work.

The finished print is peeled from the block. A single wood block, if carefully handled, can yield a few hundred clear impressions before the raised design begins to chip.

whole. Within a generation of Dürer's death his admirer, the Italian painter and art historian Giorgio Vasari, included the *Melencolia I* among the prints "which will set the whole world in astonishment." Vasari attributed the melancholy of the seated figure to the clutter of technical apparatus on the ground. Later commentators saw the *Melencolia I* as a reflection of Dürer's mood after his mother's death, and even interpreted the numbers in the square as a mathematical rebus of the death date. An 18th Century scholar felt that the woman's disordered hair was "perhaps meant as an indication of a corresponding inner confusion" and thought the instruments on the ground were the subject of her meditation, while an early 19th Century biographer attributed her "despairing" mood to the closed book on her lap.

Modern interpreters, searching more precisely for Dürer's sources in medieval and Renaissance allegory, astrology, scholastic philosophy and humanist symbolism, have proposed several more plausible keys to the *Melencolia I.* Some believe that the impedimenta of the engraving represent the seven liberal arts of the medieval schoolroom: the scribbling cherub stands for Grammar; the scales, by their connection with the law, for Rhetoric; the square, Arithmetic; the sphere, Astronomy; the compasses, Geometry; the radiating heaven, Music; the book, Logic. Others believe that the works can be explained in terms derived from astrology, with the whole picture resting under the effulgence of Saturn, the planet of melancholics. Dürer himself said that Melencolia was a woman "from whose eyes Saturn looks out." He probably derived much of his symbolism from a book, *On the Triple Life,* by the celebrated Italian Platonist Marsilio Ficino, which was published in Germany in

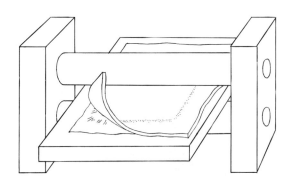

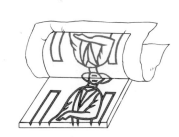

The plate and a piece of damp paper protected by a felt blanket are squeezed between the rollers of a press. Forced into the grooves, the paper picks up the inked design.

The print is pulled from the plate. Because it is more durable than a wood block, a copper plate can usually yield more clear copies before its grooves become worn.

1505. Ficino, following Aristotle, taught that "all men who excel in a great art have been melancholics." In his surpassing engraving Dürer may indeed have combined his personal melancholy with the humanist belief that the highest form of intellectual activity is found in the melancholic temperament.

Yet even when one makes no attempt to decipher the meaning of the objects in Dürer's work, the seated figure with the staring eyes remains the personification of the mysterious sadness of the world.

In 1526, two years before his death, Dürer made a summing-up of his artistic skills, of his own evolving religious beliefs, and of what he had come to understand of human nature and character, in the larger-than-life figures of his painting of *The Four Apostles (page 156)*. The execution of this diptych, with two Apostles on each panel, occupied Dürer for several years. His culminating work, it went not to any patron but to his native city as a memorial. With the completion of *The Four Apostles* Dürer's creative life approached its end. On finishing it he wrote to the Nuremberg Council:

"Prudent, honorable, wise, dear Masters. I have been intending, for a long time past, to show my respect for your Wisdoms by the presentation of some humble picture of mine as a remembrance; but I have been prevented from so doing by the imperfection and insignificance of my works, for I felt that with such I could not well stand before your Wisdoms. Now, however, that I have just painted a panel upon which I have bestowed more trouble than on any other painting, I considered none more worthy to keep it as a reminiscence than your Wisdoms."

In *The Four Apostles* Dürer broke with artistic custom by providing a religious picture for a secular setting—in this case the Treasurer's Chamber of the Town Hall. The secular quality was emphasized by the omission of the central panel—customarily a depiction of the Madonna and Child or of the Crucifixion—for which the panels of the apostles might have been expected to serve as wings. Just so had Dürer's contemporary, Martin Luther, tried to eliminate the central authority of the Universal Church and establish the direct authority of the Bible. In his left panel Dürer placed St. Peter in the background where, holding the golden keys symbolic of papal authority, he yields homage to the Book held by the luminous dominating foreground figure of St. John, who shows him the opening lines of his Gospel: "In the beginning was the Word." In the right panel a solemn and determined St. Paul grasps his book in one hand and a sword in the other. Behind him stands St. Mark. Although scarcely more than his head shows against the somber background, St. Mark is the dominating presence in this panel. Of St. Mark's Gospel Dürer said that it was as alive as if it had hands and feet. This was the power that the artist transmuted into the glowing features of his saint and into the substance of his picture.

One can see *The Four Apostles* in historical perspective as a final resolution of Dürer's own feelings, of the inner commitment he made to the cause of Martin Luther even though he remained in the Catholic Church. His contemporaries may well have seen the painting as a Lutheran manifesto. Looked at through our nonsectarian eyes, the Reformation dims. What emerges is the religious affirmation of life that each Apostle in his disparate and individual way displays.

If there is an equivalent greatness in German painting to Dürer's *Four Apostles* it is to be found in the vast altarpiece that his shadowy contemporary, the Alsatian Mathis Gothart Nithart, known as Matthias Grünewald, painted some time between 1511 and 1515 for the monastery Church of the Order of St. Anthony in Isenheim *(pages 16-31)*. But Dürer in his masterpiece shows himself the man of the new age, whereas Grünewald—although he died in the same year as Dürer—is the last of the great Gothic artists, summing up in his climactic work all the hopes and emotions of the dying Middle Ages.

Included in Grünewald's work is the most agonizing Crucifixion ever painted. The figure of the Saviour hangs from the Cross in the anguish of the death sweat, the body bruised and beaten, the greenish flesh putrescent and studded with thorns, the arms almost wrenched from their sockets, the devastated face seared by a grimacing half-open mouth from which no words come. Although rendered in the style of the Gothic, Grünewald's treatment of his theme cuts across the centuries. It reflects the recurrent tragedy of man's existence, the perennial voiceless cry against fate.

To the modern mind this tortured painting is more immediately impressive than Dürer's optimistic masterpiece, more akin to the starkness of the existentialist thought-patterns of today. Yet the two pictures are really the two sides of human nature. For if man's tragedy is in the Isenheim *Crucifixion,* man's hope is in *The Four Apostles.* As to which is the greater work, one cannot really compare the two. Each says with overwhelming power what it has to say.

Grünewald's works, aside from *The Isenheim Altarpiece,* are few, and in his isolation he stood apart from his time. Dürer's output was enormous—more than 100 paintings, more than 1,000 drawings, engravings, woodcuts, dry points and etchings—and he was so much part of his age that in many ways he came to represent it. The German conception of the Christ-image derives from him. Just as it is impossible to visualize the *Last Supper* except through the eyes of Leonardo, so one cannot conceive of the tangible figures of John, Peter, Mark and Paul except through Dürer's portraiture. Nor can one conceive of the development of Northern European art without him, though one can do so easily without Grünewald.

If Dürer had remained as obscure as his great contemporary, if nothing of his had survived but *The Great Piece of Turf,* "The Four Horsemen" of *The Apocalypse,* the *Melencolia I* and *The Four Apostles,* the power and scope of the artist would still be apparent. To understand these four pictures is to understand him. Beyond contemporary enthusiasms, fads, innovations and aberrations, there is an underlying democracy to art. What in the end endures does so because it deserves to endure. And whatever the shifts in perspective, these pictures by Dürer have endured in their common humanity over four centuries, as living now as they were in that cresting moment between the medieval and the modern era when he made them.

The Last Gothic Master

At the beginning of the 16th Century, Albrecht Dürer was infusing German art with the new spirit of the Renaissance he had absorbed on two trips to Italy. But his great contemporary, Mathis Nithart Gothart, called Grünewald, remained true to his rich medieval heritage and crowned his career by creating one of the last and most powerful expressions of the Gothic spirit—*The Isenheim Altarpiece.*

Grünewald's brilliantly colored polyptych, made for the high altar of the Antonite monastery church at Isenheim, Alsace, is a huge work, 11 feet tall and nearly 19½ feet wide. It consists of 11 panel paintings and an inner tableau of sculpture hinged together so that they can be viewed successively in three different groups of scenes. The altarpiece played an important role in the Antonite fathers' healing efforts; the sick and lame from the monastery hospital were frequently brought before it as part of their treatment. On various occasions they were shown "The Crucifixion," which appears on the outer panels; the scenes behind these, which include such joyous details as the one at right, from "The Nativity"; and the innermost group, dedicated to the monastery's patron saints.

On the following pages is a simulation of the altarpiece as the Antonites and their patients actually saw it, with instructions on how to fold the pages to re-create Grünewald's multiple masterwork.

On one of the Nativity panels of *The Isenheim Altarpiece,* a trio of angels serenades the Infant Jesus with stringed instruments; behind them, adoring seraphim float in glowing haloes of color. Grünewald artfully contrasted such joyousness with the pain and suffering in the Crucifixion scene *(overleaf).*

Grünewald: *The Isenheim Altarpiece,* c. 1511–1515. Detail from "The Christmas Picture"

How to Re-create
"The Isenheim Altarpiece"

In the photograph of a model of the altarpiece above, the central panels portraying the Crucifixion are shown slightly ajar. They may be swung open to reveal other paintings: an Annunciation, a Nativity, and a Resurrection. These, in turn, may be opened to show the shrine and two scenes from St. Anthony's life.

The diagrams at right show how the pages following may be folded to simulate the altarpiece's wings. First turn to pages 22 and 23. Lift the edges of pages 20 and 22, together, with your left hand; lay a ruler along the dashes at top and bottom center of page 22 and carefully fold and crease both pages over the ruler toward the center of the book. Do the same with pages 23 and 25. With all four half-pages folded into the center you will be looking at the Crucifixion group *(diagram A)*. The inner scenes are revealed by opening out the edges of pages 19 and 26 *(diagram B)*. Finally, to see the shrine, open out all folds so that the pages lie flat again *(diagram C)*. To insure that each group of scenes is arranged correctly, match the key letters A, B or C, which you will find at the top center of each page.

When the pages following are folded according to the instructions at right, statue-like portraits of St. Sebastian *(above)* and St. Anthony *(far right),* are seen flanking "The Crucifixion," a masterful depiction of suffering. In the central panels Christ's body slumps heavily, actually bending the arms of the Cross; His mouth hangs open; His body is spotted with the scourges of the splintery rods; His hands, expressively elongated, are contorted in a startlingly real agony.

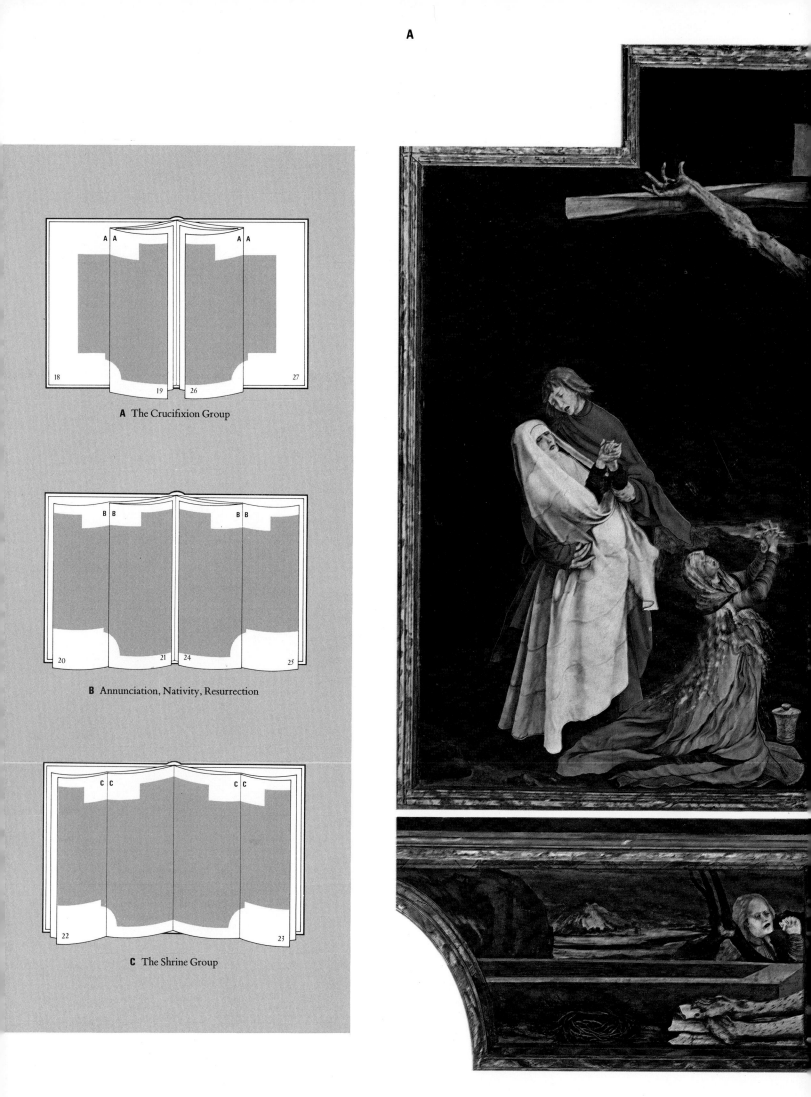

A The Crucifixion Group

B Annunciation, Nativity, Resurrection

C The Shrine Group

The Prophet Isaiah, detail from "The Annunciation"

In the second stage of the altarpiece—which depicts "The Annunciation" *(above)*, "The Nativity," usually called "The Christmas Picture" *(center panels)*, and "The Resurrection" *(far right)*—Grünewald displays his genius for color in scenes of joy, each illuminated by auras of light. At center right, the Madonna and Child, serenaded by an orchestra of angels, are bathed in the radiance that emanates from the figure of God the Father; the angels and a second figure of the Virgin, kneeling within

Lift and unfold to see details ▶

The Kneeling Virgin, detail from "The Christmas Picture"

The innermost group of the altarpiece is a shrine
containing carved portraits of St. Augustine *(left)*,
St. Anthony *(center)* and St. Jerome *(right)*,
attributed to the sculptor Niklas Hagnower. Below
is a sculptured frieze by Desiderius Beychel depicting
Christ among the Apostles. This scene is covered
by Grünewald's "Lamentation," but when the shrine
is to be displayed, the painting is detached.

22

On the left-hand panel Grünewald portrayed
St. Anthony, the patron saint of the Antonites,
meeting the hermit St. Paul in the desert. On the
right, he depicted St. Anthony beset by a host of
grotesque temptations. The pictures, which showed
the saints enduring privation and torment, were
intended to inspire the inmates of the hospital with
hope for their own cures.

Turn to pages 28 and 29
for a detail from
"The Temptation of St. Anthony"

The Christ Child, detail from "The Christmas Picture"

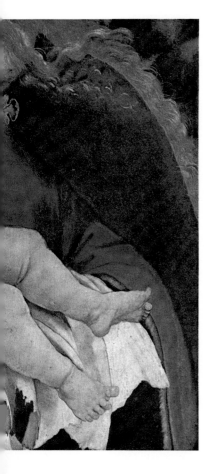

Soldier at the Tomb, detail from "The Resurrection"

an ornate Gothic tabernacle, are crowned
with brilliant haloes.

In these scenes Grünewald pictures three
different figures of Christ. The plump Infant of
"The Nativity" is held in a tattered cloth that
symbolically links Him with the dead Christ in
a loincloth in "The Lamentation" below.
On the right-hand panel *(above),* enclosed in
a sunlike halo that blinds the soldiers guarding
Him, the Saviour rises from His tomb, His
hands outstretched in a gesture of hope.

26

The Lamb with Cross and Chalice, detail from "The Crucifixion"

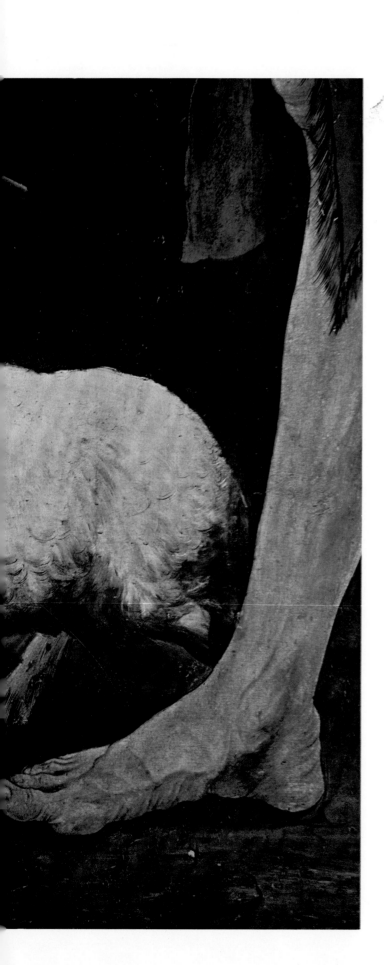

Grünewald further heightened the tension of "The Crucifixion" by creating a powerful, asymmetrical composition, placing the figure of Christ slightly off center. He added to its meaning not only by painting figures in sizes relative to their importance, but by ignoring chronology to include John the Baptist *(right)*, whose ministry had prefigured Christ's but who was already dead at the time of the Crucifixion. His resurrected presence here suggests the Resurrection of Christ.

◀ *Lift and unfold to see detail*   27

In sharp contrast to the hideous demons that Grünewald invented to represent St. Anthony's tempters *(previous pages)* are these details from "The Christmas Picture," shown in the altarpiece's second grouping. Like other elements in the paintings, the details are symbolic: the flower above suggests the Virgin, who had been described in the writings of a popular saint as a "thornless rose." The buildings in the distance are thought to symbolize both the Isenheim monastery and "the Lord's dwelling." In the detail at right from the same painting, God the Father, surrounded by His Heavenly Host, sheds a radiant and beneficent light upon the Nativity scene below.

II

Beginnings
in Nuremberg

An almost photographically precise
image of a clump of grass is one of the
meticulously rendered studies of birds,
plants and animals that Dürer made to
sharpen his powers of observation.
Although this watercolor is accurate
enough to serve a botanist—each plant
in the cluster can be identified
—Dürer's skill elevates the work to
the status of art.

The Great Piece of Turf, 1503

At the time of Dürer's birth the concept of Germany as a nation did not yet exist. While France, England and Spain were shaping their national identities under the centralizing force of strong monarchies, Germany remained a patchwork of little Germanies, more than 300 petty states and free cities in all. Physically they lay within the bounds of the Holy Roman Empire, and ostensibly they owed a common allegiance to the Emperor. But by the latter half of the 15th Century the occupant of the throne had become an emperor without substance or power, and his realm—established 600 years earlier by Charlemagne in the hope of reviving the might of ancient Rome—had long since lost any semblance of solidity. As Voltaire later observed, the Holy Roman Empire was "neither holy, nor Roman, nor even an empire."

The practical control of German affairs was exercised by assorted hands in assorted ways. Under imperial charters the 66 free cities, Dürer's birthplace of Nuremberg included, governed themselves. Outside the cities several hundred free imperial knights—lesser nobles who held hereditary feudal lands through direct imperial grant—were the absolute monarchs of their own small domains. Above them in both rank and extent of holdings were 50 ecclesiastical and 30 lay princes. At the summit of power were seven great princes: the Margrave of Brandenburg, the Duke of Saxony, the Count Palatine of the Rhine, the King of Bohemia, and the Archbishops of Cologne, Mainz and Trier. These were the Electors, so called because it was by their majority vote that the emperor was chosen. Often he might acquire his title through bribery, only to find himself faced with the hostility of the men who had elected him. Though they might war with one another, they were united in their determination to yield none of their power and possessions to the disintegrating imperial authority.

When Dürer's father came to settle in Nuremberg in 1455, a scion of the Habsburg dynasty, Frederick III, had been emperor for 15 years and was to reign for 38 more. Frederick's ambition, which he successfully realized from the first to last of his lengthy regime, was to do nothing. He himself said that he preferred to conquer the world by sitting still. All forms of physical activity were disagreeable to him, even hunting, and he rarely left his estates near Vienna. His chief interests were alchemy, astrology, and his collections of plants and precious stones. In his indolent seclusion, he cared little about the welfare of Germany and less about any efforts to reform the Empire. Yet for all his negligence he did not neglect the tradition of his Habsburg inheritance, nursing the passive hope that one day the whole world might be subject to his Austrian-based family. Optimistically he decorated his houses, furniture and books with the monogram AEIOU—*Austriae est imperare orbi universo* (Austria is to rule the universe).

While Frederick consulted the stars and carved his monograms, Germany went through a protracted period of dark unrest, ominous with uncertainty and change. Peril was ever present, both within the region's borders and beyond them. The Turks' capture of Constantinople in 1453 had done more than topple the 1,100-year-old Eastern bastion of Christendom; it had opened a road for the Moslems into Europe. The victors advanced into Belgrade and threatened to invade the Holy Roman Empire itself. Frederick shed tears at news of the fall of Constantinople, but did little else.

Inside his realm wars were endemic. The followers of John Hus, the Bohemian reformer who had been burned at the stake for his denunciations of Rome, battled traditionalist Catholics in recurrent clashes that prefigured the Reformation. Powerful families like the Hohenzollerns of Brandenburg and the Wittelsbachs of Bavaria engaged in bloody contests for territorial gain. Frederick's vassals regularly made war on one another or on the free cities. Only a few years before the elder Dürer's arrival in Nuremberg, its citizens had withstood a besieging force of several thousand nobles led by the Margrave of Brandenburg, united in their contempt for the base blood of the city's burghers and lusting for their riches. Conflicts of every sort kept breaking out in all parts of Germany, beyond the Emperor's power to control. And from their dilapidated castles the impoverished knights watched like birds of prey, ready to pounce on the unwary passing trader and hold him for ransom.

The peasants and land-bound serfs who constituted the overwhelming majority of the German population varied in their lot. Some peasants had freed themselves of feudal obligations, and in south and central Germany they were often not badly off. But a region that flourished in one decade might be laid waste the next, either by war or by pestilence. As the 15th Century progressed, the peasants' plight grew worse. Private armies destroyed their fields and burned their houses. The great princes encroached on them more and more, restricting their hunting rights, subjecting them to military service, taxing their livestock and possessions, until finally they grasped flails and reaping hooks and rose in dumb, murderous anger. In 1458 infuriated peasants besieged the Archbishop of Salzburg when, after devaluating their coinage, he demanded a tax on their cattle. Twenty years later there was to be a formidable peasant uprising in Carinthia, against the Emperor himself, that would have strong overtones of anticlericalism and radical social reform.

In the closing decades of the century it was as if the Four Horsemen of St. John's vision were again riding—this time across German fields ahead of the armies that trampled the crops to mire. Bad harvests gave way to famine; outbreaks of the plague were reinforced by the arrival of syphilis. Added to the menace of the robber knights was the grim threat of the *Vehmgerichte,* secret tribunals which claimed the right of summary judgment and execution over all the Emperor's subjects. Among the common people, harried and fearful, the belief spread that the world would end on New Year's Day of 1500, at the mid-point of the second millennium. Meteors plummeting to earth and comets streaking across the night skies were regarded as portents of the downfall of mankind and the Last Judgment.

Overwhelmed by the anarchy of daily life, many Germans found consolation in pilgrimages. Plowmen would leave their fields, blacksmiths their forges, housewives their kitchens, to make their way to the shrine of the Holy Blood at Wilsnack, where three consecrated wafers had been seen to drip blood, or to Niklashausen, where the visionary shepherd and village musician Hans Böheim claimed to have talked with the Virgin Mary. To the multitudes come to hear him he preached sermons denouncing popes and emperors, nobles and clergy, and declaring that taxes should be abolished, that land, forest and water

Dürer's Germany, as the map at left shows, was made up of dozens of separate political entities that were part of the Holy Roman Empire. Although the roads which linked these often-feuding states were unpoliced, Dürer ignored the dangers of travel and managed during his life to visit almost every important center of art *(underlined on map),* from Antwerp in the north to Venice in the south. Eventually the fragmented political units of the region were unified into nations, as shown on the modern map above.

should be made common property, and that even the great lords should be made to work for a living. Thousands of worshipers followed their "Hänselein," coming hundreds of miles to kneel for his blessing. Though Church authorities finally seized the "holy boy," and he was burned at the stake in Würzburg, singing hymns until the smoke choked him, his turbulent ideas lived on to agitate the countryside.

Only within the walls of the German towns was there anything like security. Local political conflicts—occasionally spilling over into street riots—might erupt between the craftsmen of the guilds and the oligarchy of merchants and landowners that usually controlled the governing council. Nevertheless, by comparison with the anarchy outside their gates the towns were islands of peace and prosperity, havens for the new humanist scholars as well as for skilled handworkers. Schools for the young flourished, and the art of writing—a rare accomplishment elsewhere—became almost commonplace. Municipal government developed into a stable and predictable structure, with by-laws written down and official records kept. To the soil-bound serf, the glimpse of the town behind its battlements was like a glimpse of Paradise; he was well aware of the medieval tradition that whoever could make his way inside to eat his bread unmolested for a year and a day became a free man.

Like most cities of Germany and indeed of all Europe, Nuremberg traced its origins to a fort by a river. Originally the turreted citadel on the rocks above the Pegnitz was the Bavarian stronghold of the 11th Century Emperor Henry III, who was also Duke of Bavaria. In time his successors used it simply as a base for hunting in the nearby Franconian forest or as a stopping-place en route to newer and more sumptuous castles, and it became the traditional residence of an imperial appointee called the burgrave—count of the fort. In its protective shadow the town grew up, and as the town grew, so did the walls and battlements necessary to guard the inhabitants against outside attack.

Dürer's native city of Nuremberg is seen in a panoramic view illustrating a 15th Century law book. Above the city is the imperial eagle and the coats of arms of the city and the mayor; these are flanked by St. Sebald, Nuremberg's patron saint *(left)*, and St. Lorenz, to whom two of the city's most beautiful churches were dedicated.

Nuremberg's history paralleled that of many of the cities of the Empire in its gradual evolution from a dependency of the Emperor and a private possession of the burgrave to a self-governing community rich enough and strong enough to resist all assailants. The Germans, Slavs and Franks who made up its population began to combine in a unique blend of dialect, dress and customs. Burghers became conscious of themselves as Nurembergers, proud and confident enough to engage in frequent conflicts even with their own burgrave. Finally, in 1427, the last of the burgraves, Frederick I, sold his hereditary castle to the town. Frederick, a member of the Hohenzollern family, was one of the seven electors of Germany. His adroit political and financial support had secured the imperial throne for the current incumbent, Sigismund, who had rewarded him with the margravate of Brandenburg, the vantage point from which the Hohenzollerns ultimately would make themselves kings of Prussia and emperors of Germany. Preoccupied with Brandenburg, Frederick was now willing to part with his burgravate, and the Nurembergers were willing to pay his rapacious price to rid themselves of the galling overlordship. In 1433 Sigismund gave Nuremberg a charter confirming its privileges and granting it the right to the permanent custody of the imperial jewels and insignia, as well as certain sacred relics. Nuremberg, though required to pay yearly taxes to the crown, became to all intents and purposes independent of outside authority.

Two decades later, when Dürer's father reached the city, it had a population of 20,000. It would not have seemed much of a place to modern eyes. Most of the houses were small, of lath and plaster on a timber framework, with overhanging gabled fronts and usually with thatched roofs. The narrow streets were clogged with refuse and ordure. But even a modern eye could not have failed to be struck by the imposing triple set of walls that encircled the city, with their four gates and 128 towers; the sharp towers of the churches of St. Sebald and St. Lorenz; the castle on its commanding rock; the spacious market place with its ornate fountain dominated by the exuberant late-Gothic Church of Our Lady. Contemporary travelers were impressed by the city's wealth, its prosperous textile and mining firms, the gorgeous pageantry of its festivals, the assurance reflected in its town hall, its charitable foundations, its public baths, its municipal brothel and town brewery. Visiting Nuremberg at about the time that Dürer's father arrived there, the Italian humanist Aeneas Sylvius Piccolomini—later Pope Pius II—wrote: "When one . . . perceives this glorious city, its splendor seems truly magnificent. When one enters it, one's original impression is confirmed by the beauty of the streets and the fitness of the houses. . . . The Imperial castle proudly dominates the town, and the burghers' dwellings seem to have been built for princes. In truth the kings of Scotland would gladly be housed so luxuriously as the ordinary citizen of Nuremberg."

In a city of such obvious attainments, a master craftsman could easily settle down to his trade with satisfaction. Nuremberg, straddling the north-south and east-west routes, had become a center of commerce between the Levant and Europe, and a major market for the products of Italy, drawing to itself not only craftsmen but distinguished men of learning. In the year of Dürer's birth, Anton Koberger, "the prince of booksellers," set up a printing shop that would eventually house two dozen presses, employ a hundred journeymen and make Nuremberg Europe's printing capital. That same year, the mathematician who developed trigonometry, Johannes Müller, came to Nuremberg and established an observatory. Müller, who in humanist fashion took the Latin name of Regiomontanus, after his native Königsberg, explained his move to the city in terms that could have served for many another scholar. "I have chosen Nuremberg for my place of residence," he wrote, "because there I find without difficulty all the peculiar instruments necessary for astronomy, and there it is easiest for me to keep in touch with the learned of all countries, for Nuremberg, thanks to the perpetual journeyings of her merchants, may be counted the center of Europe."

Through the Spittler Gate, under whose arches burgraves and emperors had ridden in pomp, the elder Dürer trudged in dusty solitude on St. Eulogius's Day, 1455, his tools and possessions on his back. In his obscure person, as he arrived in the heart of Germany, he was completing a cycle begun several centuries before when his nameless peasant ancestors had left their German homeland to settle or be settled in Hungary.

"I, Albrecht Dürer the Younger," his son wrote in the family chronicle he compiled about the time he was planning *The Four Apostles,* "have put together from my father's writings where he came from, how he came and remained here and went to his salvation. God be merciful to him and to us. Amen.

"Like his relatives, Albrecht Dürer the Elder was born of a family in the Kingdom of Hungary, not far from a small township named Gyula, eight miles below Grosswardein, in a little village near at hand, Eytas by name, and his family kept cattle and horses for a living."

Whether or not the Dürers had Magyar blood in their veins is uncertain. The fact is that basically they were German, always so considering themselves, speaking German, persisting in holding to their birthright in a foreign land. Generation after generation of German settlers had kept their mother tongue while living out their anonymous and usually brief lives on the Hungarian plains as cattle breeders, horsemen and miners. Sometimes they adopted the name of their trade, sometimes they found a derisive nickname fastened on them, but most commonly they took the name of the place where they lived. The Dürers derived their name from their long-since-vanished village of Eytas, a word apparently based on the Hungarian *ajtó,* or door. The Dürers found it natural to translate the Hungarian into German—*Tür*—before adapting it as a patronymic. Dürer's father signed himself Türer, and the shield he later displayed before his Nuremberg workshop—and that his son still later elaborated into a coat of arms—shows an open double door.

"My father's father was named Anthoni Dürer," Dürer recorded. "He went as a boy to a goldsmith in the said township (Gyula) and learned the craft from him. Afterwards he married a young woman named Elizabetha, who bore him a daughter, Katherina, and three sons. The first son, Albrecht Dürer by name, was my beloved father, who also became a goldsmith, a chaste and skillful man."

Anthony Dürer, after serving his apprenticeship, had set himself up as a goldsmith in Gyula in 1410. His firstborn followed his craft. The second son, Laszlo, became a bridlemaker; the third a priest. The "chaste and skillful" Albrecht was a restless young man who, after his apprenticeship was over, spent several years traveling across Europe, observing the conditions of his trade, visiting the craftsmen of precious metals in the Low Countries—then ruled by the splendor-loving Duke of Burgundy, Philip the Good—observing the marvelous Gothic flowering of the Flemish painters and finally ending his wanderings inside Nuremberg. As he passed through the Spittler Gate he was 28.

For 12 years—a long time, as his son recorded—he served the goldsmith Hieronymus Holper, and then, as was often the custom in those days, married Holper's 15-year-old daughter Barbara, "a pretty, upright maid." As Holper's son-in-law and heir Albrecht received his Nuremberg citizenship and a year later master's status in the goldsmiths' guild. He rented the back part of a house near the main market belonging to the patrician Dr. Johannes Pirckheimer, whose son Willibald would become his son's boyhood companion and closest friend.

Albrecht the Elder carefully kept his family records, and in 1471 he

Heraldry was a subject of great interest in Dürer's day, and the artist himself designed many coats of arms, including this one for his family, which he produced as a woodcut in 1523. At the top, beneath his monogram, are a pair of eagle's wings that are symbolic of strength, a Moor's head and a knight's helmet. Below these is the double-door emblem of his father's family (the name "Dürer" was derived from the German word *Tür,* meaning "door"). Dürer also used the double-door emblem as a seal on his letters.

noted: "Item, in the sixth hour of St. Prudence's Day, on a Tuesday in Passion week (May 21) . . . my wife Barbara bore me a second son, to whom Anton Koberger was godfather, and called him Albrecht after me." That Koberger, the printer and publisher, should serve as godfather was a sign of Dürer's rise in the world from the wandering craftsman of 1455. The boy Albrecht was the third of 18 children, most of whom did not survive childhood. His mother, who died in 1514, lived long enough to bury 13 of them. Of her in after years her son wrote: "She often had the plague and many other severe and strange illnesses, and she suffered great poverty, scorn, contempt, mocking words, terrors and great adversities. Yet she bore no malice. . . . She feared Death much, but she said that to come before God she feared not."

A son's love exaggerated the harshness of family conditions, for the elder Dürer—far from being scorned—was a "juror" and later "street captain" of a respected guild, a man honored by appointment to the goldsmiths' office of inspection and to the position of assayer to the mint. Nor could a craftsman, however thrifty, be considered poor whom the Emperor patronized and called "my goldsmith," and who received orders for silverware from the town council and commissions from such patrons as the bishop of Posen and Nuremberg's Holy Ghost Hospital.

"My father endured much and worked hard all his life," his son wrote, "for he had nothing for his support save what he earned with his hand for himself, his wife and his children. . . . He led an honest God-fearing life, and was a gentle patient man, friendly to all and thankful to God. He cared little for company and nothing for worldly amusements. . . . He told us every day that we must love God and be honest in our dealings with our neighbors."

The background of most 15th Century painters is indeterminate, but one can learn minutely about the Dürers from their carefully kept family chronicle, and one can still see the pious, limited, honest, careworn parents in their portraits. The father appears in a silverpoint drawing of about 1486, once thought to be by the hand of the young Albrecht, but now considered more likely a self-portrait. The elder Dürer is wearing work clothes and a brimless felt hat; his craftsman's firm hand holds a small metal figure. His face is prematurely old and lined. A thin mouth turns down at the corners, gray hair curls unkemptly from the edges of the hat, and the narrow steady eyes are those of the craftsman who does not look beyond his trade.

The character of the mother appears in an almost life-size charcoal drawing of her head made by her son shortly before her death. One can trace death's presence in the emaciated face with its long nose, wrinkled forehead and bony features. It is a sad, exhausted face cross-hatched by sickness, care and grief, with only the great luminous eyes untouched by the harshness of life, as if they themselves were looking beyond life.

These portraits do much to explain Dürer's inheritance: from the father the skilled, careful hand, from the mother the visionary outlook. Combined with an inner intensity of genius—in itself not to be explained —these qualities were to make this Nuremberg craftsman's son the artist of his country and his age.

Severe portraits of Dürer's parents reflect the years of toil that marked their lives. The drawing of the senior Dürer, holding a statuette symbolic of his goldsmith trade, is probably a self-portrait. Dürer himself made the striking charcoal sketch of his mother two months before her death. On it he later inscribed: "This is Albrecht Dürer's mother; she was 63 years old and she died in the year 1514 on Tuesday before Rogation week about two hours before night."

Dürer's Precursors

German art in the century before Dürer, like German politics of the time, was largely regional and provincial. Just as there was no strong central government in Germany, there was no dominant artistic movement. In Flanders, Jan van Eyck had achieved a brilliant reputation with the new technique of oil painting; in Italy, a variety of talented artists had developed the laws of perspective that altered the course of painting. But in Germany art remained fragmented for many years.

German regional painters continued to rely on local traditions that were largely medieval, as the work at right shows. Among the clues to this heritage are the artist's condensation of several moments in time, the vivid contrast in scale between figures, partly based on their social status, and a careful attention to physical detail.

However, the artists of Germany had not always been entirely isolated from outside forces. In the late 14th and early 15th Centuries, a new artistic style had developed. Born in the courts of France and transmitted through Flanders and Italy, the so-called International Style crossed borders freely in the form of easily transported illuminated manuscripts and small panel paintings. Reflecting the increasing secularization of art and the growth of a class of wealthy private patrons, the elegant style spread widely. German artists adapted it in charming scenes filled with local color, setting the stage for a broader employment of foreign influences.

This painting, from a multipaneled altarpiece, illustrates part of the legend of St. Barbara, a medieval martyr who was slain by her father for converting to Christianity. Here, the haloed saint is seen hiding in a forest as her father questions a pair of shepherds who saw her vanish. (The noble and his henchmen are painted as oversized figures as a mark of their rank.) In this panel Barbara is being betrayed by a shepherd—who is immediately punished by having his flock turned into grasshoppers.

Meister Francke: *Pursuit of St. Barbara*, c. 1415

Master of the Middle Rhine: *The Garden of Paradise*, c. 1410

Bright colors, strong linear patterns and a lyrical tone characterize German paintings influenced by the courtly International Style. Although the works shown here reveal their Gothic character, especially in the expressive elongation of the figures, something strikingly new has appeared. In the scene above, by an artist known only as the Master of the Middle Rhine, the subjects seem to be lords and ladies in a castle garden. But they can be identified as the Virgin *(top, center),* the Christ Child (playing with St. Cecilia and her zither) and St. Michael, St. George and a third knightly saint in the group at right. The garden was thus a symbol of Mary and her virginity. This secularization of art occurred as stable local governments assumed powers formerly exercised by the Church.

In the mid-15th Century, a new concern with three-dimensional reality appeared in German painting. Stephan Lochner showed his awareness of space in the painting at right, in which the foreground figures are clearly larger than those in the background and a new emphasis on picturing deep space is evident. Although still true to his Gothic heritage and the decorative qualities of the International Style, Lochner—whom Dürer admired—was pointing the way to a new phase in German art.

Stephan Lochner: *The Adoration of the Child*, c. 1445

To later painters, the conquest of reality became ever more important. The Swiss Conrad Witz, who painted Christ walking on the Sea of Galilee while His apostles draw up the miraculous netful of fish (*below*), exploited familiar regional details to make his scene seem real: the shore of the Biblical sea looks like Lake Geneva; Swiss villages dot the lakefront. Even the fishermen and the reflections in the water around their teetering boat give a sense of immediacy and reality.

Michael Pacher, a Tyrolean sculptor-painter, achieved realism in another, equally effective manner. Fascinated by the Italian experiments with perspective, Pacher toward the end of the 15th Century became interested in manipulating space. His altarpiece panel at right reveals how well Pacher understood the concept of foreshortening—especially evident in the cradle—and how to achieve depth by using light and shadow. His painting of the canopy and niche enclosing St. Ambrose is an almost sculptural rendering of forms. Through men like Pacher and Witz, German art, though highly regional and slow to change, gradually moved toward a new realism and pictorial power on which Dürer would build.

Conrad Witz: *Christ Walking on the Water*, 1444

Michael Pacher: Panel from the *Altarpiece of the Four Latin Fathers*, c. 1483

III

"The Wander Years"

Dürer was 19 and just past his apprenticeship when he portrayed his father in oil, perhaps to display his new skill in painting. The elder Dürer, wearing a fur-lined jacket and holding a rosary, has the look of a man who, as his son later noted, "had little need of company and worldly pleasures."

Albrecht Dürer the Elder, 1490

When Dürer was four years old his father bought a large house in Nuremberg known as Unter der Vesten (Below the Fortress). Here, three doors from the bustling studio of the painter Michael Wolgemut, he set up his goldsmith's shop and hung out a sign bearing the double-doored Dürer shield. The printer Anton Koberger, young Albrecht's godfather, had his presses close by; the physician-chronicler Hartmann Schedel, the calligrapher Johannes Neudörffer, and the humanist writer Christopher Scheurl all lived in the neighorhood.

For a few years Dürer learned reading, writing, arithmetic and the rudiments of Latin at the St. Lorenz grammar school. But since his elder brother had died, it was taken as a matter of course that Albrecht as the next son would follow in the family craft, and so while still a child he took his place as an apprentice in his father's shop. There he became familiar with the engraver's tool, the burin, practicing the minutely exact workmanship of the goldsmith's art, unwittingly training his hand and eye for the time when he would make engravings on copper.

Almost daily he must have passed Wolgemut's workshop and glanced through the door with excitement at the busy scene: the younger apprentices mixing colors, cleaning brushes or preparing wood panels; the older apprentices and assistants painting the details of some large altarpiece as it had been outlined by their choleric, parrot-nosed master. Wolgemut was the first artist of Nuremberg to turn painting into an industry by using many hands for work ostensibly his own. His shop output was enormous. Orders poured in from churches and monasteries, but in his collectively competent style he was able to meet the demand.

Wolgemut had been the pupil of a greater painter, Hans Pleydenwurff, whose shop he had taken over at the older man's death in 1473 and whose widow he had married. Pleydenwurff had brought two major innovations of the Flemish painters Jan van Eyck and Rogier van der Weyden to South Germany in his religious pictures: he substituted figures with lifelike movement and glowing colors for the stylized, stiff-draperied figures of the older Franconian school, which flourished in South Germany, and he replaced the plain gold backgrounds used by the older painters with realistic landscape backgrounds that might even include the familiar steeples of Nuremberg. Wolgemut accepted the Flemish background innovations but drifted back to the earlier Franconian tradition for his figures. With his mass-production methods he was unable to give as distinctive a style to his work as did Pleydenwurff. Nevertheless he enjoyed great contemporary fame, and there could scarcely have been a better place than his workshop for an eager boy to learn the techniques of painting.

As the inscription in the upper right-hand corner states, this oil portrait by Dürer of his painting master, Michael Wolgemut, was done in 1516. Three years later Wolgemut died, and Dürer added the words: "And he was 82 years old and lived until the year 1519, when he passed away on St. Andrew's day (November 30), early, before the sun rose."

Dürer's innate quickness to learn had already made itself apparent in his father's shop, and afforded the elder Dürer a special pleasure in his second son. But for all the boy's facility with the burin his heart was not in making chalices and gold and silver ornaments. "My liking drew me rather to painting than to goldsmith's work," he later recorded. "I put this to my father but he was unhappy, for he regretted the time lost while I had been learning the goldsmith's craft. Nevertheless he gave in, and on St. Andrew's day, 1486 years after Christ's birth, my father apprenticed me to Michael Wolgemut, to serve him three years. During that time God granted me diligence so that I learned well, though I had to endure much from the shop boys."

Workshop hazing and horseplay were hard on any novice, and the younger the novice the harder the life. But though Dürer looked back on his apprentice years with less than nostalgia, he was never to lose his feeling of affection for Wolgemut, whom he called his "second father" and whom he portrayed in oil with much tenderness and sympathy three years before the old man's death in 1516. As an apprentice he practiced the techniques of handling pen and brush, and learned to use oils and to draw and copy from life. He also had his first encounter— one which would be so vital to his future—with woodcuts. This still-primitive art form was less than a century old, but Wolgemut had appreciated its possibilities early in his career, and had refined and developed it to the point that he and his stepson Wilhelm Pleydenwurff were preparing illustrated books in collaboration with their printer-neighbor Anton Koberger. The most splendid result of their efforts was the hundreds of illustrations for Hartmann Schedel's *Chronicle of the World,* a comprehensive history that was one of the most copiously illustrated books printed up to that time. Dürer observed and possibly even aided in its preparation.

The young apprentice, certain of his desire to be an artist but still uncertain of the way he must take to reach that goal, found himself awed and moved to emulation by the widely circulated engravings of two artists: the Flemish-influenced Alsatian, Martin Schongauer, and a Dutchman of uncertain name, known as the Housebook Master for the pen-and-ink drawings with which he illustrated a text containing rules to guide a Master of Arms in running a noble household.

The spiritedly original Housebook Master, who had come to Germany in the last quarter of the 15th Century and settled in the region of the middle Rhine, was the first artist to use the technique of dry point. In this form of engraving the artist makes his design on metal by scratching it with a needle instead of gouging out a smooth line with a burin. A print from such an engraving is less precise than a line engraving and has an informal, almost velvety appearance. With his subtle needle the Housebook Master scratched on lead, rather than on the usual copper, the droll and engrossing figures from everyday life that people his prints, drawing them with a humorous realism that was in deft contrast to the controlled and highly finished technique of the traditional engraving. For his religious engravings as well as in his pictures of everyday life, the Housebook Master used the people about him as models. His soldiers were the soldiers one saw on the road, his burghers those of any German town.

However much the young Dürer admired the Housebook Master's work—his haunting dry point *Death and Youth (page 56)*, particularly, seems to be reflected in Dürer's emergent art—it was Schongauer whose work he cherished most deeply and imitated most faithfully until he was ready to stand on his own. Starting out in life, like Dürer, as an apprentice to a goldsmith father, Schongauer had become the greatest German artist of his time. It was primarily through him that the severe Gothic realism of the Flemish north filtered into Germany in a softer form. Gentleness and strength, a serene otherworldliness, made him the Fra Angelico of the north. In his engravings he depicted the life of Mary, the sufferings of Christ, the Apostles, the wise and foolish virgins *(page 58)*, in fact all the conventional medieval themes of the art of the time; but he transformed them with his mild radiancy.

Schongauer's engravings followed the course of the trade routes, scattering across Europe like autumn leaves. Nuremberg shops and workshops were full of them. They were imitated in France, Spain and Central Europe; in Italy the young Michelangelo copied in oil Schongauer's engraving of *The Temptation of St. Anthony.* Dürer himself would later use many of the details of Schongauer's *Flight into Egypt* in his own *Flight into Egypt,* part of a series of woodcuts devoted to the life of the Virgin. Poring over Schongauer's engravings in the Wolgemut workshop, the apprentice determined that when his time was up he would make his way to Colmar in Alsace and work directly under the revered master.

The pen drawings that survive from Dürer's apprentice period—among them a Crucifixion, a battle of horsemen, a soldier taking aim with a crossbow, a cavalcade of fashionable young people—show the rapid ripening of his talent. Even more extraordinary are the three watercolor landscapes that date from this nascent period—*Wire-Drawing Mill, The Cemetery of St. John's,* and the *Three Linden Trees.* Dürer's handling of perspective is awkward, but he has recorded the scenes with a visual exactness amazing for a boy: the compact arching trees, with the lower leaves already beginning to fade in the summer heat; the city wall, the church and the lambent countryside beyond; the unrippled reflection of the river by the mill, the very texture of brick and tile and timbering in the high-pitched peasant houses, have all been rendered in sensitive detail.

Dürer marked the formal conclusion of his apprenticeship at the age of 19 by painting twin oil portraits of his mother and father. He used the

Wolgemut's Nuremberg studio, where Dürer worked as an apprentice for three years, was located in the building at the far left in the photograph above, just a few doors from Dürer's father's house, at far right. The original buildings were heavily bombed in World War II but have been rebuilt since.

traditional form of a diptych, with the mother in one frame and the father in the other, looking obliquely at each other; and on the back he sketched two coats-of-arms—the open door of the Dürers on a triple mountain in gold on a red ground, and the rampant ram on a blue ground of the Holpers, his mother's family. The left section with his mother's portrait has vanished, and one can judge the diptych only by the portrait of the father *(page 46)*, holding a rosary and dressed now in his Sunday best instead of in the work clothes in which he had been depicted five years before. But the portrait has the same tired, irregular features and thin mouth of the earlier sketch, and the eyes look not so much toward his wife as back into himself. Caught by the son's loving insight, it is a face for which life will have no more surprises.

Dürer left Nuremberg in April 1490, on his *Wanderjahre*, or "wander years," the period of traveling that young German craftsmen who had finished their apprenticeship customarily undertook before settling down. Upon the advice of his father, who remembered his own travels, Dürer spent a year and a half journeying all over Germany on his way to Schongauer's Colmar workshop. Just what his route was, and how long he spent where, remain matters of speculation. He may have seen or tried to see the Housebook Master near Frankfort, he may even have gone north to the Netherlands as his father had done in his own wander years. The only biographical note that has survived is a quick sketch he drew of himself in 1491 on the back of a more formal drawing of the Holy Family he had made earlier that year. It is a brooding face, perplexed almost sullen, unformed yet passionate, the face of a boy still bewildered by life.

Dürer arrived at the Rhine somewhere in the neighborhood of Frankfort early in 1492 and followed the river south to Colmar—only to discover that Schongauer had died the year before. Schongauer's brothers, the goldsmiths Caspar and Paul and the lesser painter Ludwig, received him with "benevolence and humanity"; but the workshop was by now in decline, and there was little for him to do and less to learn, so the Schongauers recommended him to their fourth brother, Georg, a respected and prosperous goldsmith who was a resident of Basel, 40 miles up the Rhine. Seizing the opportunity, Dürer moved on.

Georg welcomed the young man with the same openhanded hospitality that the rest of his family had shown. The Swiss city had become a center for the publication of sumptuously illustrated books, and Dürer undoubtedly had introductions from his godfather Koberger to two great publishers of Basel, Nicolaus Kessler and Johannes Amerbach. The newcomer must have made a good impression on Kessler, for in an edition of the *Letters of St. Jerome* the old printer allowed the unknown young man to make a woodcut of the saint for the title page. By luck, the block itself still survives, bearing the signature "Albrecht Dürer von Nörmergk" on the back, and it is the one woodcut of the artist's Basel stay that can be assigned to him without question. (It is one of the relatively few blocks carved by Dürer that still exist.) This woodcut of the long-nosed St. Jerome drawing a thorn from the paw of a lion appears crudely executed when set beside Dürer's later work—the lion

Almost everything he saw, including his own image, was a suitable subject for the young Dürer's pen, and he never tired of drawing from life. This sketch, made when he was 22, includes a study of his own hand as well as one of his first full-face self-portraits. Even a pillow could fascinate Dürer: he would draw one, as above, thump it to give it a new shape, and then draw it again; this detail is one of seven pillow sketches he made at one sitting.

looks more like a poodle—but it represents a noticeable advance over Wolgemut's technique.

From internal evidence of style and by comparison of content with later works, scholars have tried to identify other woodcuts of Dürer's Basel sojourn. It seems highly probable that he designed a number of the illustrations for Marquart von Steyn's moralizing treatise, the *Knight of the Tower,* and Sebastian Brant's angry social satire, *The Ship of Fools.* But this can never be proved with finality, any more than it can be proved that—as some observers believe—the St. Jerome figure of the woodcut was suggested by a portrait of the late Swiss master Conrad Witz, who had lived in Basel and whose paintings and drawings Dürer must have studied there.

After Basel, his farthest point south, Dürer went north again, to Strasbourg. There in that thriving city of many printing shops, with its great rose-colored cathedral dominating the Alsatian plain, he lived until the spring of 1494. It is not known where or for whom he worked; one scholar has suggested that he made friends with the painter Hans Baldung Grien, then still an apprentice, who would later come to Nuremberg and work in Dürer's studio; but there are very few details available about this sojourn. Nevertheless, it is a curious footnote that the most German of German artists should have come to that very city where three centuries later the young Goethe would re-create German poetry and where, in his circle, German nationalism with all its subsequent grandeur and misery would be born.

Despite the lack of documented information about Dürer's stay in Strasbourg, some paintings and drawings from the time of the visit still exist. Two self-portraits, one a pen sketch and the other a finished oil, are particularly interesting. The sketch shows him in the same pose as in the sketch of two years earlier, but the brooding, uncertain boy's face has now acquired a scrutinizing glance that glows with assurance. With this assurance, Dürer seems older than in the more formal oil done the same year. Here the face of the not-yet-mature young man looks, even with its slight fuzz of an incipient beard, almost feminine. There is an elegance to his dress, a certain aristocratic carelessness in the slender blue-eyed figure. The tassels of the red cap, set jauntily aslant his head, seem almost part of the texture of his curling blond hair. He wears an elegant gray jacket edged with braid, and his finely pleated shirt is fastened by six rose-colored ribbons. In his hand he holds a kind of thistle known as Mannstreu—a symbol of man's fidelity.

There was a special significance in the symbolism of the Mannstreu because back in Nuremberg arrangements had just been made, in the custom of the day, for Dürer's marriage. In the spring of 1494 the elder Dürer had been approached by the respected craftsman Hans Frey to arrange a marriage between Albrecht and Frey's 15-year-old daughter, Agnes. The Freys were several cuts above the Dürers in the social world of Nuremberg, being related to a patrician family, a connection that secured Frey various municipal offices and a place on the 200-member Grand Council. Frey had started out as a coppersmith, then turned his talents to the whole field of metalwork for which the city was

The earliest woodcut attributed to Dürer shows St. Jerome in his study pulling a thorn from a lion's paw; it was used as a frontispiece for a collection of St. Jerome's letters published in Basel in 1492. In the woodcut, the open books with Greek, Latin and Hebrew texts refer to Jerome's great achievement, the creation of a complete Latin Bible from ancient sources. Dürer's improbable rendering of the lion may be explained by the fact that at the time he had never seen a live one.

so noted, producing armor, astronomical instruments, music boxes and the small pocket watches now known as "Nuremberg eggs." His prosperous workshop was particularly noted for its ingenious portable mechanical fountains, popular as table decorations in wealthy houses.

Frey must have been impressed by young Dürer's talent to propose the match with his daughter. He also offered a handsome dowry of 200 florins. The elder Dürer agreed and the contract was signed before the usual witnesses. The goldsmith now sent for his son. No doubt Dürer, in Strasbourg, painted his self-portrait as a likeness sent in advance for approval. On it he wrote in acceptance of his prearranged fate: *"Myn sach die gat als es oben schtat"*—"My affairs are going as ordained on high."

Dürer was married to Agnes Frey on July 7, 1494, less than eight weeks after his return to Nuremberg. It was to be a childless marriage and an unhappy one. A pen sketch that he made of "my Agnes" at the time of their wedding shows a small sober face, with the spring charm of youth but no great beauty. With the schoolgirl's pigtail that she wears and her modestly plain clothes, she seems from another world than that of the elegant young man in the red-tasseled hat. Later, however, she would grow into an intimidating female. Though her husband wrote with much affection of his mother and father, he was never to write about his wife at all.

It was customary at that time for a newly wedded burgher couple to live a year with the bride's parents. Dürer, however, took his young wife to his father's house, and they lived there briefly while Dürer established himself in Nuremberg's intellectual community, and began a pattern of behavior that would be characteristic of their whole married life. It was the familiar pattern in which a husband continues to expand his horizon, to grow intellectually and socially, while his wife remains at home, static and sullen.

Agnes had no doubt thought she was marrying a man like her father or her father-in-law, craftsmen rooted in their shops and restricted in their social life to their trade and work associates. Instead she found herself, while still a girl, linked to a restless-minded artist who found an outlet for his energies in the company of scholars and scientists rather than in a wife and home (he seems to have had no other loves). By the time he was 25, Dürer had become mature and articulate enough to mix easily with patricians and nobles, bishops and men of learning in a world that would always remain alien to Agnes. Isolated both intellectually and physically, lacking the satisfaction of children, she grew bitter, and hated the diversions that kept her husband apart from her. Above all she detested her husband's worldly patrician friend Willibald Pirckheimer. Pirckheimer returned the feeling, and after Dürer's death—in a letter to a friend—he accused her of bringing her husband to an early grave through her testy, avaricious nature. "Nagging, jealous, shrewish," Pirckheimer called her.

Pirckheimer's boyhood friendship with Dürer, unlikely though it at first seemed within Nuremberg's stratified society, was to grow with the years. Each friend sustained the other. Pirckheimer was a convivial man-about-town, a lover of sport, a widower with a weakness for women but no intention of giving up his freedom for a second time; on the other hand, he had also studied law and the humanities in Italy at the great universities of Padua and Pavia, and was a humanist and a poet, one of Nuremberg's most learned citizens. He initiated Dürer into the Greek and Latin classics, kept him informed about new trends in philosophy and discoveries in archeology, even suggested subjects for prints. Dürer in his turn illuminated books in his friend's library, drew his portrait, designed a bookplate for him, illustrated his writings and gave him his company.

Within a matter of weeks after his return to Nuremberg, Dürer's friendship with Pirckheimer and other scholars had drawn him into the intellectual excitement being produced in Germany by the ferment of the Italian Renaissance.

In the field of scholarship, the Renaissance spirit had already taken over the studies of Northern Europe. Medieval Latin—so-called Low Latin—though it had been a living language and an international medium of communication among literate men, was now scorned by scholars, who preferred instead the formal correctness of the classical prose of Cicero and Seneca. Pirckheimer and his humanist acquaintances would have derided the Latin lyrics of the preceding centuries, wry and charming though they were, because of their unclassical meters and rhyme patterns.

In art, however, this Renaissance preoccupation with ancient themes had not yet penetrated. Painters and engravers still produced the religious pictures, Biblical themes and scenes of everyday German life that had concerned their medieval forebears. The realism of Flemish art had made its impression, as in the work of Pleydenwurff, but the neoclassicism of the south had been ignored. Dürer, with his questing mind and close relationships with classical scholars in Nuremberg, was by temperament and opportunity prepared, as no other German artist had been, to respond to the warm Renaissance winds from the south.

At Wolgemut's studio he saw prints and engravings by such Italian masters as Mantegna and Pollaiuolo that were arriving over the Alps. In them Dürer caught a glimpse of the classical themes and techniques that were inspiring Italian art, and they must have been a revelation to him. He copied several Mantegna engravings—among them the *Battle of Sea Gods* and *Bacchanal with Silenus*—apparently sensing in them the ancient freedom of form and expression that had so long been inhibited by the spirit of Scholasticism. At a distance he understood that Italian artists, with their revived interest in classicism, were demolishing restrictive medieval canons. Increasingly he became aware that the realization of his own art lay in the south, in the capturing of form, in the technical knowledge of proportion and perspective, in the study of body structure.

In the late summer of 1494, Nuremberg was struck by an outbreak of the plague that recurrently swept Europe's cities. This may have spurred Dürer's decision. In any case, less than two months after his marriage, he set off for Italy, alone.

Dürer painted his first self-portrait in oils (*above*) at the age of 22. Dressed fashionably and sporting a tasseled cap, he seems self-confident, although he was only on the threshold of his career. The work was finished not long before his marriage, which may explain why he holds a thistle, symbol of marital fidelity. The sketch of his wife Agnes (*below*) was done in the year after their marriage. Although Dürer often painted his own portrait, he seldom portrayed his wife. Of the few pictures of her that survive, this is the earliest and the most flattering.

Pioneers of Printmaking

Three technological innovations of the 15th Century were to have profound repercussions not only on history, but, more specifically, on the art of Albrecht Dürer. The first was the invention, in about 1450, of movable type—individually carved or cast letters—that could be printed in combination with illustrations cut on wood blocks. The second, and intimately related, innovation was the development of cheap methods for the manufacture of paper, which had formerly been imported at great cost from the Far East. The rapid and economical multiplication of printed, woodcut-illustrated pages—sold singly or bound into books—stimulated an appetite for words and pictures that has never been satisfied.

At first, woodcuts were made by craftsmen employed by publishers who printed and sold their work. Gradually, however, artists of greater skill brought a new sophistication to the medium. The woodcut at the right, for example, was created by Michael Wolgemut, a noted painter who was Dürer's first teacher.

The third innovation was the improvement of the printing press so that designs incised into metal plates, called engravings, could be printed. Engraving began as an offshoot of the goldsmith's skilled craft and as a result, early engravings are often finer than woodcuts of the time. The art evolved quickly in the hands of talented men like the Housebook Master and Martin Schongauer, whose work set a model for Dürer.

With two fingers raised in the traditional gesture of the Creator, a majestic God causes Eve to rise from Adam's rib. This early woodcut is from a massive book called *The Chronicle of the World*, for which Michael Wolgemut and another artist created over 650 illustrations. Although the design lacks refinement it has undeniable energy and dramatic force.

Michael Wolgemut: *The Creation of Eve*, c.1490

One of the finest early engravers was an anonymous artist known as the Housebook Master because scholars have linked his work with drawings in the same style in a manuscript called the *Hausbuch.* The engravings shown here illustrate a variety of subjects: a traditional religious scene *(right),* a parable on death *(left)* and an amusing, true-to-life observation *(below).*

The method employed by the Housebook Master is called dry point, a technique he pioneered. In dry point a fine needle is used to scratch the metal plate, raising a burr alongside each line. This burr traps ink and, when the plate is printed, a soft, delicate line results.

Informality pervades the Housebook Master's subjects. In the scene at right, for example, Joseph is shown playfully tossing apples on the ground to amuse the Christ Child. At left, the artist treats the widespread medieval preoccupation with death, usually portrayed as a grotesque specter, by juxtaposing a gaunt but gentle old man and an elegant youth—a reminder that life is short and beauty fades.

The Housebook Master: *Death and Youth,* c.1480-1490

The Housebook Master: *Dog Scratching Itself,* c.1480-1490

The Housebook Master: *The Holy Family*, c.1480

Martin Schongauer: *A Wise Virgin*, c. 1480-1490

Martin Schongauer: *A Foolish Virgin*, c. 1480-1490

Martin Schongauer was the first great engraver to sign his works—each of the three shown here bears his monogram. Unlike the Housebook Master, Schongauer used the conventional engraving technique, whose deep, continuous lines, incised with a chisel-like engraving tool, suited his more elegant, form-defining style.

Among Schongauer's most influential works is a series of 10 small engravings illustrating the New Testament parable of the Wise and Foolish Virgins. Artists of Dürer's time found inspiration in Schongauer's graceful feminine figures, two of which are shown at left, and his audience readily appreciated their symbolism. In the parable, 10 maidens, each of whom carries a lamp, are going to a wedding. But the bridegroom is late and by the time he arrives, five of the maidens, who have neglected to bring oil for their lamps, find that they will not light. These maidens are not admitted to the wedding.

To Schongauer's contemporaries, the wedding was understood to represent the Kingdom of God. The arrival of the bridegroom was seen as the Second Coming of Christ, and admission to the wedding was viewed as the Last Judgment. Thus, the faithful maidens—those who were prepared with oil and who were called Wise Virgins—were admitted; the impious Foolish Virgins were turned away. Schongauer's portrayal of a weeping Foolish Virgin *(left, below)*, with her unlit lamp turned sadly upside down, is a charming image.

More dramatic is Schongauer's engraving of *The Temptation of St. Anthony (right)*, a popular subject that would later inspire Grünewald *(page 23)* and other artists. For his version Schongauer invented a battery of fantastic animal demons to beset the saint, who remains calm amidst their torments. In addition to Schongauer's imaginative creatures, the engraving shows his superb control of his medium: through stippling, hatching and precisely cut lines the artist has rendered a variety of textures and shapes. It was this aspect of Schongauer's work that especially influenced his young countryman, Dürer.

Martin Schongauer: *The Temptation of St. Anthony*, c. 1480–1490

1503·

IV

An Awakening in Venice

Long before Dürer's time Italy had become—and for centuries afterward remained—the visionary country of the Germans. From their northern land of chill autumn mists and brutal winters and late springs, they dreamed of sunshine and landscapes where the fruit glowed like lanterns in the dark green foliage of the orange trees. Three hundred years after Dürer, Goethe would sum up the persistence of the German vision in his "Mignon's Song" as an inextinguishable *Sehnsucht nach Italien,* a "longing for Italy."

In the late 15th Century a rich patrician like Dürer's friend Pirckheimer could make the dream actual in his well-upholstered travels to some Italian university town, but for a working German artist to make his way alone and on foot over the Alps for the sake of perfecting his art was still unheard of. After Dürer the artist's journey to Italy would become a tradition, then a commonplace, finally a persisting cliché, so that even in the 19th Century no self-styled artist, whatever his land of birth, would consider himself such unless he had studied there. Artists of the young American republic, like Washington Allston, were drawn to Italy by the same feelings that had drawn Dürer—if not with the same result.

When Dürer set out from Nuremberg in September 1494, it was natural for him to pick Venice as his goal. Not only was it the nearest large city across the Alps from Germany—no inconsiderable matter for anyone making his way on foot—but it was an established commercial center where for 300 years German merchants had sent their products in exchange for the spices and silks and luxury goods brought to Venice from the Orient. Much of the wealth of the leading Nuremberg families had come from the profitable Venetian trade, and all the more important Nuremberg merchants were represented at the Fondaco dei Tedeschi, the warehouse of the Germans near the Rialto Bridge, which served as both their trading and social center. The merchants even operated their own postal service to Venice, sending couriers who made the trip over the Brenner Pass in 10 days.

Dürer spent a leisurely month wandering along the same route on his way south, following the highway to Augsburg, reaching the Alps at

While visiting Venice in 1494, Dürer made many copies of the muscular nudes that pervaded the work of Italian artists. The main outlines of the pen-and-ink drawing below, for example, were traced directly from one of Andrea Mantegna's engravings (detail above), which shows a fight between two mythological sea creatures. One important difference in their drawing techniques can be seen, however, for where Mantegna indicated shading with straight parallel strokes, Dürer used subtle curves to create depth.

Mittenwald and Austria at Innsbruck. After the gentle countryside around Nuremberg he found the jagged mountain scenery overwhelming. Everywhere in the bright September weather, now slightly misted, he stopped and sketched the ephemeral moment. These sketches he intended for future reference, and indeed many of the scenes served as background for his later prints. Through the drawings that survive—some of them done on the way south and some on the homeward trip—one can trace the course of his travels. At Innsbruck he drew the town from the bank of the River Inn, using muted autumn colors—gray-green water, a gray-blue sky and the snow-streaked mountains, brought to life by the vivid and contrasting red of the tiled towers. He also sketched the angular courtyard—perspective was obviously still giving him trouble—of Innsbruck Castle, then occupied by the Habsburg prince and Emperor-elect Maximilian, who was later to be Dürer's devoted patron. The watercolor, now lost, that Dürer made of the mountain town of Chiusa, south of the Brenner Pass, he would use as the setting for his engraving of *Nemesis*. He also recorded the walled town of Trent, showing it in a wide curving valley by a placid river, with the blue and amethyst haze of the mountains in the background.

When Dürer reached Venice in October 1494, the opulent city was trembling on the edge of its decline, although neither he nor its pleasure-loving citizenry could have known this. Only four years later the Portuguese navigator Vasco da Gama, sailing around Africa to India, would open a new route to the Orient and thereby bring about the ultimate destruction of Venetian dominance over trade with the East. But in 1494 Venice was still Queen of the Adriatic. For Dürer it proved a revelation, a vast expansion of his horizon. Accustomed to Nuremberg's limiting walls and battlements and the surrounding Franconian forest, he beheld a semi-Oriental city whose only boundaries were the sea, whose population numbered four times that of Nuremberg. Instead of a crowded jumble of narrow jutting houses, there were spacious open palaces painted in gold and ultramarine before which were anchored brightly decorated ships from many lands. Instead of the muted tones of the angular buildings of the North, there were glittering veneers of dark red porphyry and green marble on domed churches. The exotic mystery of Byzantium lurked just beneath the Gothic traceries of the basilica of St. Mark's.

Philippe de Commines, the envoy of Charles VIII of France, who arrived in Venice at the same time as Dürer, recalled his impressions of the city in his memoirs: "I was taken along the High street, they call it the Grand Canal, and it is very broad, galleys cross it . . . and it is the fairest street, I believe, that may be in the whole world, and filled with the best houses. . . . The ancient ones are painted . . . and most have a great piece of porphyry and serpentine on the front. . . . It is the most triumphant city I have ever seen, and does most honor to ambassadors and strangers."

Dürer found Venice equally congenial. His taste for elegance, evident in his betrothal self-portrait, was gratified by the city's luxury. Absorbing the urbane manners of the South, he soon became a young *gentiluomo,* like the local dandies who promenaded on the Rialto and the Piazza San Marco. Immersed in the city's dazzling pageant, he filled his sketchbooks with fragments of its abounding life. Always intrigued by textures, he drew the gorgeous dresses of Venetian women; in one double drawing he contrasted a *gentildonna* in her loosely fitting dress with the coifed figure of a Nuremberg *hausfrau.* He sketched courtesans and Oriental slave girls, turbaned Turks, animals, the stone lions of St. Mark's, classical figures and landscapes. The fish market with its weird creatures from the sea fascinated the land-bound German as it would later fascinate Goethe. In watercolor he recorded a baleful-looking crab and a giant lobster with one distended claw, painting them with a zoological exactness that nevertheless suggests the fantastic creatures of Hieronymus Bosch.

Venice, with its links to the East and its preoccupation with trade, was less affected than other Italian cities by the artistic stirrings of the Renaissance. Unlike Rome or Florence it had few antiquities that could be viewed directly. Dürer pursued his classical explorations mostly by studying the engravings of Mantegna and Pollaiuolo. In copying these works, he emphasized the muscular play of the mythological nudes they featured and often achieved a greater intensity and expressiveness than could be found in the originals.

Dürer took pains to learn the anatomy of the human body; probably he received instruction in drawing from life. Studying the "naked pictures of the Italians," as he put it, was indeed a primary purpose of his visit. While still in Nuremberg he had become convinced that the Italians had rediscovered rules of bodily symmetry and proportion that had "been lost and hidden for more than a thousand years," rules that might be reduced to some precise geometric formula describing the perfect human form. "I found no one who had written of any such thing save one man, Jakobus by name," he wrote, "a good, amiable painter, born in Venice, who showed me the figures of a man and woman which he had drawn in proportion." Jakobus was a minor painter, Jacopo de' Barbari, whom Dürer gratefully and grossly overrated. His supposed geometric method launched Dürer on a lifelong search for a formula that would explain human movement and proportions. Though Dürer would never succeed in this search, his progress in understanding the subtleties of the body after just a few months in Italy is evident in the contrast between an awkward naked peasant girl he sketched in 1493 and a regal Venetian nude leaning gracefully on her staff that he drew two years later.

At that time, the foremost artist of Venice was the 65-year-old Giovanni Bellini, the brother-in-law of Mantegna. Dürer soon found his way to the large studio that Bellini and his older brother Gentile had inherited from their father. The brothers ran their studio much as Wolgemut operated his workshop in Nuremberg, using many assistants and producing large numbers of religious paintings. Titian and Giorgione were apprentices of the Bellini at the time of Dürer's visit, but there is no indication that he met them.

The Bellini made Dürer welcome. Gentile let him sketch a group of

Dürer was fascinated by animals and grasped every opportunity when traveling to make realistic sketches of those he was not able to find in Nuremberg. This watercolor study of a crab was made on the artist's first visit to Venice in 1495. Every joint of the creature's legs and claws is rendered with precision.

The many modes of dress of the cosmopolitan Venetians intrigued Dürer, and during his sojourn in their city he made several costume studies. This one contrasts a Venetian woman's garb *(right)*, with that of a Nuremberger. Dürer's eye for detail is seen in his emphasis on the differences between the two styles: the German dress with its tight bodice and elaborately draped skirt, the Italian with high waist and long straight skirt resembling a classical column.

Turks that he himself was using as models for a picture, and he allowed him to copy a profile portrait he had made of the ex-Queen of Cyprus. Dürer learned much from Giovanni's austere yet glowing Madonnas, framed by landscape backgrounds as serenely unified as they were natural. No doubt through his study of these works the German visitor came to understand that in art a landscape is a unity greater than the sum of its parts, a lesson he was to apply on his way back to Nuremberg.

The half year that Dürer spent in Venice took him to the threshold of his maturity. How much these months refined his technique and widened his concepts can be seen in the watercolors he painted on his journey home. He followed a leisurely route back in the spring of 1495, passing through Padua and Verona and along the edge of Lake Garda until he rejoined the courier road at Trent. As Dürer left Venetian territory, he stopped near the border to paint a view of the hill fortress and village of Arco that he called *Fenedier Klawsen,* "Venetian mountain pass." Although house, tree and tower are as sharply defined as in an engraving, the individual objects are submerged in the vibrant atmosphere of the spring morning. With the silver-blue pattern of the olive trees, the first thrust of the leaves through the clipped grape vines, one can almost hear the echoing call of the cuckoo through that lucid air. The exact formula for human proportion might continue to elude Dürer, but in this view of a flat-roofed village under a jutting peak, with the road behind the peak winding into infinity, he demonstrated clearly that he had grasped the secret of aerial perspective.

Somewhere in the mountains east of Trent, Dürer painted a view of the South Tyrol that he called *Wehlsch Pirg,* "Italian mountain" *(pages 74-75).* This sunset view of a tranquil valley, indicated in the broadest strokes, with its cultivated fields and its village and the sharply defined mountain beyond, has gone past the limitations of architecture and detail. No longer does Dürer use color merely to fill in drawn outlines; now color absorbs the outlines and itself creates form. Here is the breathing earth caught in the timeless moment before the light fades. This awareness of air and light, of the landscape as a thing in itself, was the beginning of the European feeling for landscape that developed over the next three centuries. The freedom and expressiveness of Dürer's watercolors would be particularly reflected 300 years later in the sketches of the Englishman, John Constable.

On his return home, Dürer applied his new understanding of landscape to his own countryside, and saw it with a new vision. A watercolor sketch, *Pond in the Woods,* was painted in the sandy heathland a few miles from Nuremberg. The subject is no more than a small pond banked by sedges, with straggling conifers near a sand bar on one side and a line of dead trees on the other. The setting sun shows a sudden burst of orange against lowering purple-to-gray clouds that are reflected more darkly in the shallow water. The calm landscape against the violent sunset seems to sum up in the fading light the poignancy of time's passing, and the insignificant pond has through Dürer become the ideal pond in the Platonic sense.

Another watercolor, *House on an Island in a Pond,* shows what may be another inlet of the same pond. In the foreground a skiff with oars is beached near a waterlogged stump, while on an island knoll a sharp-roofed house like a miniature tower, such as Nuremberg patricians built for summer houses, is reflected in the unruffled water. Here the twilight is more advanced. The sun has already set, leaving only a streak of orange in the sky. Though the profusion of other colors—yellow, blue, violet, red and green—is muted, there is the same sense of the past moment recaptured.

Dürer also painted a view of Nuremberg from the west, where a dirt road winds across a misty summer landscape to the walled town and its vaguely outlined castle, that indicates how far he had progressed from his carefully constructed earlier watercolors. Where previously he had spent hours of draftsmanship in setting down the almost stage-prop architectural details of a scene, he was now able to submerge the details with a few unifying strokes of the brush. One senses a kind of pantheism in these later watercolors, almost a deification of nature.

Dürer confided to Pirckheimer that he was studying and making notes on landscape painting. But he considered it a minor matter. What he might have done if he had gone beyond his Gothic inheritance to become a pure landscape painter is suggested in the watercolor sketches he made in Kalchreut, a village not far from Nuremberg. He painted the village, the steep-thatched farmhouses among their ancient linden trees and the valley itself with a geometrical arrangement of color and mass in a panoramic sweep that suggests Cézanne in its modernity. No landscapes comparable to these would be painted for three centuries.

The five years that followed Dürer's return from Venice were intensely productive. During that time he drew, sketched and painted Biblical themes, philosophical and religious allegories, and scenes—often satirical—of everyday life, in a style that combined the modern manner of the Italians with the Flemish and German traditions. He produced a dozen paintings, more than 25 engravings, seven single woodcuts, the 15 woodcuts of the *Apocalypse* series and the greater part of a series of 12 woodcuts depicting the Passion of Christ. This series, as distinct from two others he later produced on the same theme, is called *The Large Passion (pages 104-105)* because of the size of the woodcuts.

After a few months of working with Wolgemut, Dürer set out to establish his own studio with his own assistants. Then, in April 1496, he met the Elector of Saxony, Frederick the Wise, who was on a four-day visit to Nuremberg. The meeting, however brief, brought the young artist his first real taste of success. Instantly impressed by Dürer, the 33-year-old Elector not only sat for his portrait, but also ordered an altarpiece, a triptych, for the chapel in his castle at Wittenberg.

The forthright Frederick, the most esteemed of the German Electors, was to remain Dürer's patron for the rest of his life. A pious man as well as a lover of the arts, Frederick was as interested in supporting painters as he was in collecting pictures. Dürer's portrait reveals a bearded, hawk-nosed man with singularly prominent eyes. Although there is no inscription or insignia to indicate the sitter's rank, one senses the commanding presence, the easy assumption of authority.

Visiting Gentile Bellini's studio in Venice, Dürer made a sketch *(below)* of three Turks who appear in the background of Bellini's painting, *Procession of the Holy Cross (detail above)*. Dürer altered the composition slightly, depicting the men as beardless and making one of them a Negro. The awkward handling of the Negro's draperies is often cited as evidence that Dürer had not yet achieved total mastery of his art.

Beset by an outbreak of the plague in 1503, Nurembergers were further terrified by a concurrent phenomenon called a blood rain, now thought to have been caused by rain-borne red algae. This watercolor by Dürer recorded the resulting stains on a servant-girl's linen shift. Apparently the algae spread out along the weave of the dress, leaving what seemed to be a crucifix flanked by ghostly figures. Dürer, awed by what he believed to be a miracle, noted that the girl was so overwhelmed "she feared that she would die of it."

Frederick's patronage contributed immensely to Dürer's reputation. Shortly after he finished the Elector's portrait, members of the Haller family commissioned him to paint a Madonna for their private chapel in Nuremberg. The Haller Madonna has so much the character of Giovanni Bellini's Madonnas, stiff yet at the same time natural, that for many years the picture was attributed to Bellini. The Child Mary holds, however, is no *bambino* but rather a German infant with long fair hair.

Neither Frederick's admiration nor the patronage of patricians was as instrumental in advancing Dürer's career as his own great project during this period, the *Apocalypse* woodcuts. It was this astonishing work, coupled with the unprecedented reproduction possibilities of the printing press, that spread Dürer's name across Europe. Even today he is remembered beyond all else for these 15 woodcuts illustrating the last book of the New Testament. Published in 1498 together with the Biblical text, in both a German and a Latin edition, they mirror much that is significant about both Dürer and his time: the first stirrings of the Reformation; the psychic shock of two conflicting worlds, North and South; the recurring sweep of the plague; the gathering feeling of doom as the year 1500 approached; Dürer's own dismay at the troubled time in which he lived, itself an echo of the time described in the Book of Revelation when "the sun became black as a sack-cloth of hair, and the moon became red as blood; and the stars of heaven fell unto the earth."

Dürer shared the credulity of his day far more than did his humanist friends. When, for example, in 1501 and for several years after, a blood-red rain (now thought to be caused by harmless algae) stained the clothing of men and women with what they imagined to be the sign of the Cross, Dürer drew such a cross that had appeared on a little girl's linen shift, considering it "the greatest miracle which I have ever seen."

The *Apocalypse* woodcuts represented the outward form of his inner forebodings. Neither commissioned nor suggested by anyone else, they seemed virtually to compel his efforts. The story of the Revelation of St. John, the Christian Jew imprisoned on the Aegean island of Patmos at about the time of the Roman Emperor Domitian, had haunted the minds of many generations before Dürer's with its fevered visions of doomsday. Pictorial renditions of these visions had first appeared in Spain in the Eighth Century in the commentaries of St. Beatus, then had spread to England and Northern Europe. The Cologne Bible of 1478 contained woodcuts of certain scenes from the Apocalypse. In Nuremberg, a Bible printed by Anton Koberger in 1483—the so-called German Bible—used the borrowed wood blocks of the Cologne edition for illustrations. But Dürer was the first to present such illustrations as a balanced series of pictures. That he had studied the Cologne woodcuts is clear; he adopted the general scheme and even many of the details of their Apocalypse scenes. But the refined woodcut technique with which he clothed his borrowed models reveals all he had learned not only from Wolgemut, but also from Schongauer's sophisticated engravings. Dürer's woodcuts show a highly developed graphic style of great richness and variety, remarkably decorative in its curvilinear treatment and black-and-white patterning, and charged with emotional vitality.

To avoid detracting from his illustrations and yet at the same time to create a real picture-book, Dürer printed the text on the reverse of his woodcuts, each plate on the right-hand page facing a text on the left. The text he used was that of Koberger's Bible, and the type face was one cut five years before for the printing of Schedel's *Chronicle of the World*. Although the words "Printed in Nuremberg by Albrecht Dürer" appear at the end of the series, this was merely to indicate the publisher and place of publication. Dürer was never a printer, as some historians have suggested, and the actual printing was probably done by Koberger.

For all their Biblical content Dürer's *Apocalypse* prints are completely Germanic in feeling. Despite his newly absorbed landscape imagery, his new understanding of anatomy and the techniques he had learned in Italy, he did not depart from his German inheritance; instead he brilliantly applied his new knowledge to it. Like Leonardo's *Last Supper* or Michelangelo's Sistine Chapel ceiling frescoes, these woodcuts, once one has seen them, seem so inevitable that one can no longer conceive of them as not existing. Giving expression as they did to the hopes and agonies of their age, they are the instinctive response of the artist to the spirit of the time. Dürer himself could not have explained why he was so drawn to the mystical Book of Revelation with its words of prophecy, because its spirit was part of the atmosphere he breathed. All his artistic gifts were poured into this series, and in the spare exactness of its woodcut lines he was able to give corporeal form to the bloody and overwhelming visions, the sense of doom and salvation, the horror and hope of his world.

To measure Dürer's accomplishment one need only read the Biblical text and then turn to his illustrations. By an extraordinary act of creative condensation he managed to distill the entire content of the Apocalypse into 15 scenes. Throughout the series one senses the undercurrent of his Italian journey. The dynamism of his relentless angels would be impossible without Mantegna. Much of the scenery echoes the Tyrol; there is even a distant glimpse of the dome of St. Mark's. In the first of the woodcuts, in which the stern and sensual-faced Emperor Domitian watches while St. John is boiled in a cauldron of oil, the Emperor is dressed as a Turk, in just such a costume as Dürer had seen and sketched in Venice. So also had he seen and sketched the Venetian lady in her loosely graceful robe before he transformed her into the whore of Babylon in the next-to-last *Apocalypse* scene. Yet these Italian traces, for all their stylistic importance, are as incidental to the impact of the pictures as is the recurring appearance of Pirckheimer's plump face in the various crowd scenes.

The first woodcut, called the *Martyrdom of St. John*, serves as a frontispiece for the visionary scenes that follow. In the next print *(page 100)* the saint, after his ordeal, kneels in new-found rapture among seven golden candlesticks before the God who, in the words of Revelation, had eyes that "were as a flame of fire. And he had in his right hand seven stars: and out of his mouth went a sharp two-edged sword: and his countenance was as the sun shineth in his strength." Such ecstatic imagery would seem impossible to translate convincingly into a pictorial medium, yet Dürer has done so with such literal exactness and such conviction that it is almost hard to believe that St. John's words ever existed without Dürer's pictures.

The 13 scenes that follow are subordinate to the primary vision of John kneeling before God. In the third print the door of heaven is opened to him—literally a double door, much like that of the Dürer family shield. The 24 elders in white, with crowns in their hands, form a luminous semicircle around the throne of God, while in the narrowed curve between them and the throne seven lamps of fire burn above the four winged beasts representing the Evangelists, with heads of a lion, a man, an eagle and an ox. Beside the throne the Lamb with seven horns and seven eyes stands on its hind legs and paws at a seven-sealed book in God's hand. Though fire and wind burst from heaven, the earth below still basks in the serenity of summer. Hill, wood and castle lie torpid in the sunshine, while skiffs glide across the calm waters of what could be Lake Garda in Northern Italy.

It is in the next woodcut, after the Lamb has opened the first four seals, that the Four Horsemen ride forth, in all their terrifying purposefulness, to trample the earth *(page 101)*. Then, in the following three prints, the remaining seals are opened. Angels proclaim the day of wrath with shattering trumpet blasts. The earth is convulsed, the sun turns black and the moon bloody. Incendiary stars rain from heaven. Popes and kings are overwhelmed along with ordinary mortals. In the seventh scene *(page 102)*, a third of the land is burned up; a third of the sea turns to blood, engulfing the ships; the star Wormwood streaks down on an errand of demolition like a comet. Great hands emerge from a cloud to hurl a flaming mountain into the sea, while swarms of scorpion-tailed locusts fall through the air like hail and a black eagle soars above the destruction crying woe to the inhabitants of the earth. In the eighth scene, the four avenging angels, merciless in their purity, wield their swords against the doomed third of mankind, while pursuing riders appear through the clouds on fire-breathing horses with the heads of lions and the tails of serpents.

The heart of the cycle is reached in the ninth woodcut, where the angel gives John the book to devour. In the language of the Apocalypse, the angel is described as being clothed in a cloud, with a rainbow upon his head, "and his face as it were the sun and feet as pillars of fire"— a description that would seem to defy translation into any linear equivalent. Yet, Dürer, following the text precisely, has produced a picture in which the glowing angel with the sunburst face, cloud-body and feet of flaming columns is actualized with vivid force and no trace of incongruity.

There is, however, a certain incongruity in the figures that populate the next five woodcuts—the woman clothed with the sun and crowned with stars, and with the moon under her feet; St. Michael fighting a turbulence of dragons; the seven-headed beast rising out of the sea; the whore of Babylon sitting on the beast with the seven heads. However plausible they may have appeared to Dürer's vision-haunted contemporaries, to modern eyes they bear a certain jarring resemblance to the mock monsters created by Walt Disney and Dr. Seuss.

With the fall of Babylon and the opening of the Book of Life, peace returns to heaven and earth and an angel, in the calm aftermath, leads St. John to his glimpse of the New Jerusalem. In this final print *(page 103)* Dürer returns from the swirling domain of the supernatural to nature and the earth. In the lower right-hand corner the chained Satan being led away to the bottomless pit by the angel with the key looks no more formidable than any bad-tempered watchdog. The apocalyptic gold-and-crystal city with its walls of jasper and sapphire and emerald is visualized by Dürer as an idealized Nuremberg lying placidly behind its walls and battlements. A flock of birds flies over, as if to emphasize the peaceful scene, and equally peaceful boats move across a mountain-fringed lake in the distance. Nuremberg and the Holy City, in Dürer's earthly conception, are at last one—or at least might be.

As soon as they were published in 1498 the *Apocalypse* woodcuts became bestsellers, circulating not only throughout Germany but in France, Italy, Spain, and even Russia. In 1502, Hieronymus Greff, a Strasbourg printer, brought out a pirated edition. Illiterates, scholars and painters were equally affected by them. The drawings of Hans Burgkmair in Augsburg, and later of the rising painters Hans Holbein in Basel and Lucas Cranach in Wittenberg, would all reflect their influence.

By producing these woodcuts on his own, Dürer had taken a unique step in art. Until then no artist had thought of undertaking a major work that was not commissioned by some wealthy sponsor. Dürer, impatient at the length of time required to execute an oil painting and at the custom of haggling over the price, had decided to free himself of the caprices of patrons by the large-scale production and sale of his woodcuts and engravings. He marketed them himself or contracted with agents to dispose of them in other cities. His wife even ran a print booth at fairs and his aged mother once took charge of a special "bargain sale" at Nuremberg's annual Relics Fair, when the robes and scepter and sword of the Emperor Otto were placed on display.

The *Apocalypse* woodcuts were intended for the mass of ordinary people. Similarly the sheets of Dürer's *Large Passion*—some of which he was working on at the same time as the *Apocalypse* series—and later his woodcut series of *The Small Passion* and of *The Life of the Virgin (pages 106-107)*, were also printed in large quantities to be sold at fairs and carnivals and distributed by agents all over Europe. So, to a certain extent, were his engravings, although essentially these were esoteric works intended for a humanist elite, an aristocracy of taste and scholarship.

Although Dürer as an apprentice had studied Schongauer's plates, engraving was a technique unfamiliar to Nuremberg, and even though he had learned to handle the burin in his father's shop, he did not begin to experiment with drawing on copper until his return from Italy. As if to develop his hand, he first turned to small engravings of such subjects as a galloping rider, a loutish cook and his wife, a rustic pair, a Virgin and Child, and the Housebook Master's theme of a young couple threatened by death. Dürer's first great picture in the new medium was *The Prodigal Son amid the Swine (page 110)*, a unique theme for him since he never again attempted the same combination of the rustic with the emotional. In his engraving the field described in the Bible story has become the barnyard of a derelict Franconian farm. Tattered and despairing, the Prodigal kneels on a dung heap. While pigs and shoats thrust round him, he calls out to God. In his abject dignity, among the decayed buildings, he has come to embody all the misery of peasant Germany.

This straightforward engraving became instantly popular across Europe and beyond. Italians copied it and recopied it. It even became a model for a Persian miniature. In Florence the art historian Vasari wrote admiringly: "In another print Dürer represented the Prodigal Son who kneels after the fashion of a peasant, wringing his hands, and looks up to heaven, while some swine feed from a trough; and in it there are hovels after the fashion of German villages, most beautiful."

But Dürer also produced a sophisticated collection of subtle allegorical engravings that were intended specifically for a more learned audience. For Pirckheimer and his other friends he created a number of highly enigmatic engravings on themes inspired by Italian art and classical Renaissance literature; it was a point of pride to devise themes that, as he himself said, "had never been in anyone's mind before." Unlike the woodcuts, which, however subtle, were generally clear in their message, the meaning of many of these engravings is still unresolved. Among the most enigmatic are *The Four Witches, The Dream of the Doctor, The Sea Monster* and the fate-picture that ranks with Dürer's half-dozen greatest, *Nemesis.*

There are distinct echoes of the Italian Three Graces in his *Four Witches,* but the theme has been transmuted to a sinister confrontation of four naked women who, as they stand in a circle, seem wholly dedicated to evil. Neither the skull underfoot nor the lurking devil in the background is needed to emphasize their malevolence. They are comely in their heavy-bodied Teutonic way, but there is nothing erotic in their nudity. It is impossible to determine what they are up to. Yet seeing them, one almost believes in witches.

The Dream of the Doctor, also called "The Temptation of the Idler," raises many more specific questions in the viewer's mind. A middle-aged man dozes beside a stove while a winged devil blows in his ear with a bellows and a lushly naked woman stands near extending her right hand in invitation to him. To her left in the foreground a winged cherub is trying to walk on a pair of stilts. What is this well-fleshed Eve doing, and why? What is the devil blowing in the sleeper's ear? What is the meaning of the cherub, or the stove, or the stilts? The questions have had many answers, perhaps the most reasonable being that the picture is an allegory of sloth. The idle man by the stove is being tempted by the devil to the sin of lasciviousness. Yet other interpreters have seen the sleeper as Pirckheimer, and the allegory as a disguised reference to his gout or—more realistically—to the syphilis that he was known to have contracted.

There are even vaguer answers to the riddles of *The Sea Monster (page 111),* which incongruously combines a classical motif with a medieval background. A merman, bearded, virile and old, and antlered like a sea god, has abducted a naked girl and is swimming downstream with her. He holds her easily with one hand, while she, perched on his broad scaly tail, turns her head away in feigned reluctance. On the far bank a small figure in Turk's costume—possibly her father—waves his arms in protest while nude bathers near him show complete unconcern. Behind the bank a Gothic fortress looms up under the shadow of a more distant turreted castle, and fair-weather cumulus clouds drift across the summer sky. What can be clearly inferred from this strange work, except that sea and summer are elementals against which is set man's ancient virility and a woman's reluctance before the unknown?

Aside from the animal-filled engraving of St. Eustace *(page 112),* the engraving called *Nemesis (page 113)* is the largest Dürer ever made, measuring about 13 by 19 inches. Like the later *Melencolia I,* to which it seems akin, it conveys its inherent meaning directly and at once, however enigmatic its details. This winged figure of a nude woman no longer young, with curved back, heavy thighs, protruding buttocks and a face of contemptuous dignity, is the embodiment—as no classical figure could possibly be—of the inscrutability of fate. In her left hand she holds a bridle and bit representing punishment, and her right hand extends the golden chalice of reward, but her feet rest on the sphere of fortune that supports equally punishment and reward. Below her the clouds roll back like a curtain to reveal an Alpine landscape in miniature pattern—the very village and valley of Chiusa that Dürer sketched on his Italian journey. Against the vastness of fate the smallness of the world lies exposed, and the unpredictability of men's destiny is revealed, as in the words of Ecclesiastes: "Time and chance happeneth to them all."

The Elector Frederick's patronage had made Dürer a fashionable painter in his native city, and from 1497 on, Nuremberg's leading citizens came to sit for him. Among others, he portrayed half a dozen members of the patrician Tucher family, painting them in the Flemish manner with an extended landscape background. One of the most striking of his surviving Nuremberg portraits is of the young and temperamental merchant Oswolt Krell, whose restless spirit Dürer stressed by the red cloth background that frames his head.

In 1498 Dürer, at the age of 27, again painted his own likeness, his first known self-portrait since the engagement picture of 1493. Once more he is dressed elegantly, with a low-cut pleated shirt of the finest linen trimmed with gold brocade, puffed sleeves of black and white, a cape held casually in place by a blue-and-white cord. On his hands he wears gray kid gloves and on his head an elaborate black-and-white tasseled cap. His earlier wisp of a beard has grown full, if not bushy, and his shoulder-length hair—then the fashion—is carefully arranged in small curls. His mouth is fuller, surer, and he looks at the world with the confident detachment of a man who has a position in it.

The portrait, with its glimpse of a Tyrolean landscape background, is the self-image of an aristocrat. Until then the artist in Germany had been a guildsman, a paint-splotched artisan in his shop, at the social level of Dürer's contemporary, the Nuremberg cobbler-poet and legendary meistersinger, Hans Sachs. In this picture of himself, and for the first time in Germany, Dürer asserted the claim of the artist to be a *gentiluomo,* equal to any man.

Dürer's first powerful patron was the Elector of Saxony, Frederick the Wise, who had acquired his nickname not through his own learning but through his encouragement of the scholarship of others. The last of Dürer's portraits of the Prince *(above)* captures not only his warmth and robust charm but also his authority. It was completed only a year before Frederick's death at the age of 62.

The Painter's Eye

Dürer produced only about a tenth as many oils and watercolors as drawings, woodcuts and engravings, but in painting no less than in the graphic arts his mastery was undeniable and his choice of themes wide-ranging. With equal facility he painted altarpieces and other religious works, landscapes and portraits, including many studies of himself; he was among the first artists in history to find his own features a recurrent source of fascination and a ready inspiration for his brush.

He took both an exalted and an intensely practical view of painting as an art. Those who excelled in it in the past, he reminded young hopefuls, had been honored by mighty kings because they were thought to possess "a creating power like God's." On the other hand, Dürer could distill the essence of painting in this terse formula: "To paint is to be able to portray upon a flat surface any visible thing whatsoever."

Dürer allowed very little to elude his painter's eye, whether he was at home in Nuremberg or on journeys to Italy and the Low Countries. Plant life, terrain, animals, people's faces and clothing—familiar or exotic —all caught his attention. So did the techniques of other artists, including the exquisite precision of Netherlandish painters and the glowing color and ordered compositions of the Italians. Everything he saw affected his painting. Late in life he could say with complete satisfaction: "Sight is the noblest sense of man."

Dürer's predilection for animals led him to surround the Virgin with a bevy of amiable beasts, in a unique treatment of the Madonna theme. This ink drawing, heightened by watercolor, may have been a study for a painting he never finished.

Virgin with a Multitude of Animals, 1503

Wehlsch Pirg, 1494

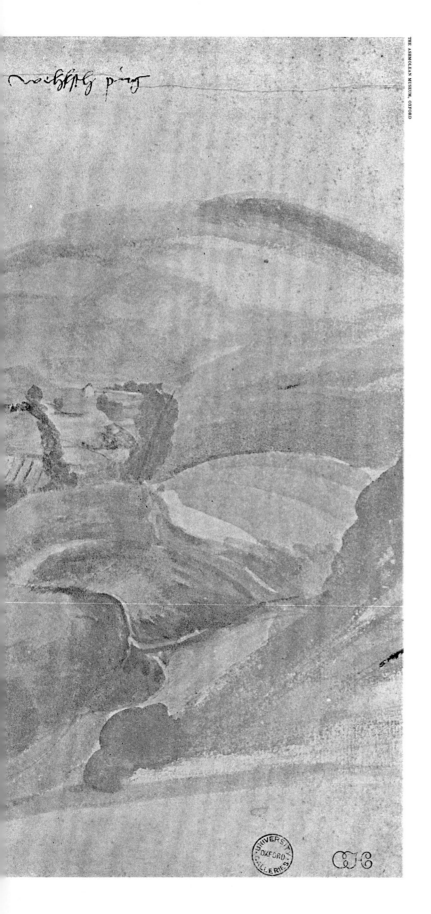

Crossing the Alps en route to and from Venice in 1494 and 1495, Dürer made abundant use of his watercolors, pausing to paint vistas that particularly appealed to him. Most of these he depicted in precise detail; the Tyrolean landscape at left, however —called *Wehlsch Pirg,* Old German for "Italian Mountain"—was a remarkable exception. Although the mountain itself is carefully rendered, the hills and valleys in the foreground are brushed in broadly, suggesting the terrain without sharply defining it.

By contrast, the *Young Hare (below),* painted by Dürer almost a decade later in his Nuremberg studio, shows a devotion to almost microscopic detail. In a tight crouch, with ears erect as though sensing the approach of a hunter, the hare is so finely delineated that even the subtle difference in the textures of the fur on the body and on the ears is clearly perceptible. As was his practice with works that satisfied his own high standards, Dürer signed and dated this watercolor.

Young Hare, 1502

The central panel of an altarpiece whose wings have since been removed, this *Adoration of the Magi* was painted by Dürer after his first visit to Venice, and shows the powerful impact of Italian ideas on his work. Like many Italian pictures of the period, Dürer's painting can be diagramed geometrically: its structural core is a triangle formed by the line of the Madonna's back, running up to the trees atop the ruins at center, thence down toward the right through the Moor and along a paved step to the foreground. The central figures—the worshipful old king and elegant young king as well as the Madonna and Moor—are linked through color and emotional contact in balanced relationships that unify the composition as a whole, producing the blend of order and drama that was an Italian hallmark. In this personal interpretation of the lessons he had learned in the South, Dürer achieved what one scholar has called "the first fully and clearly organized picture in all German art."

Adoration of the Magi, 1504

77

Portrait of a Young Girl (in Milanese Dress), 1505

Portrait of a Young Woman, 1506

Dürer returned to Italy in 1505, after having spent 10 remarkably productive and successful years in his native Nuremberg. During his stay in the South he received commissions for many portraits, among which is a charming portrayal of an elegant young girl with reddish-blond hair *(opposite)*. Painted soon after the artist arrived in Italy, the picture clearly reveals Dürer's control of the line in the crisp rendering of the girl's fine hair and the sharp delineation of her features. In contrast to this emphasis on line is the technique employed in the lovely painting above, which Dürer produced the following year, toward the end of his stay in Venice. Here, the lady's face is softly modeled, its delicate contours evoked with light and shadow in subtle shades of harmonious color. Few other works so clearly show the contributions of the Venetian masters to Dürer's art.

The Feast of the Rose Garlands, 1506

Study for Pope's Robe

Portrait of an Architect

Dürer's countrymen living in Venice were as anxious to employ him as the burghers of Nuremberg had been. Soon after his arrival, a group of German merchants commissioned the artist to prepare the altarpiece shown opposite for their church, San Bartolommeo. The subject agreed upon was a traditional Madonna and Child scene called a "Rosenkranzbild," or rose garland picture. In both style and content Dürer successfully blended characteristics of German art with the ideas of the Italians whose work he so admired.

Seated before a rich green canopy supported by two cloud-borne cherubs, the Madonna places a rose wreath upon the head of Maximilian, ruler of the Holy Roman Empire, while the Christ Child rewards Pope Julius II, leader of the Church of Rome, with a similar garland. This division of blessings between church and state reveals the theme of the painting, the universal brotherhood of Christianity. To the 15th Century worshiper, the garland was analogous to the rosary, whose beads form a circle just as Christianity encompasses all men.

Dürer planned his picture with great care. The delicate drawings above were made as preparatory studies for the Pope's robe and the figure of a local architect who stands at the far right in the painting. Dürer included portraits of other prominent German citizens of Venice among the group at the right, standing behind the Emperor. Many are portrayed so precisely that scholars have been able to identify them. Dürer also included his own self-portrait; he is standing in front of the tree at the right. He holds a scroll on which he inscribed the proud fact that he had completed the picture in a very short time.

Christ among the Doctors, 1506

These paintings, executed in Venice, reflect Dürer's fascination with human beauty, and its opposite, the grotesque. The picture above—which some scholars think was influenced by Leonardo da Vinci's well-known caricatures of aged and ugly men—contrasts the radiant countenance of the young Christ with the wrinkled visages of the doctors. Although the work is brilliant as characterization, Dürer's aim was to portray the difference between the true Christian word, as exemplified by the innocence of the empty-handed Christ, with the pedantic word represented by the books clutched by the doctors.

Dürer completed this picture in only five days, a fact that he noted on a small slip of paper stuck into a book held by the doctor at the left. And in contrast with his normal method of working, the paint is applied in broad strokes, almost spontaneously, with great freedom. The composition of the work is unusually crowded; menacing faces peer out of the background; the attitudes of figures divert the viewer's attention in several directions. None of the Italian orderliness that had so recently impressed him is noticeable. Dürer chose a simpler arrangement in composing the two elegant panels at the right, his conceptions of Adam and Eve. In these paintings he revised an ideal of physical beauty that he had created in an earlier engraving *(pages 108-109)*. There, the figures are muscular and statuesque. Here, the sinuous contours of the bodies and the soft modeling of flesh mark Dürer's new view of the human figure. The slender, elongated forms, in which the whole figure is expressed as a unity, represent yet another stage in the artist's pursuit of perfection.

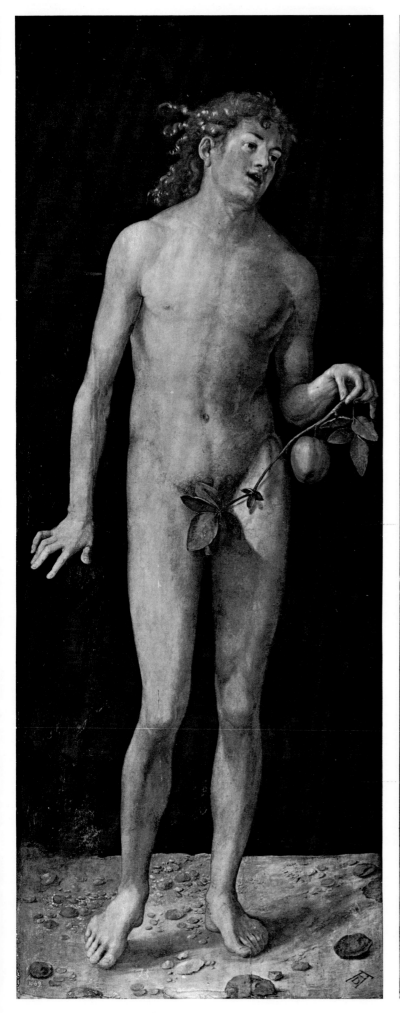

Adam and Eve, 1507

83

After Dürer's return to Nuremberg in 1507, the Elector Frederick the Wise, a long-time patron, commissioned him to paint an altarpiece depicting the barbaric mass execution of 10,000 Christians by a Persian king. Dürer had already made a woodcut of the subject but now he illustrated the gruesome event in glowing colors. In the detail at the left and in the full work below, the innocent Christians can be seen as they are hurled off cliffs, axed, stripped, decapitated, flogged and bludgeoned. In the lower left-hand corner of the picture Dürer painted a Crucifixion, evidently to link Christ's fate with the group martyrdom. And as he had done before, he included himself at the center of the picture, accompanied by a man who resembles his friend Willibald Pirckheimer. Dürer may have meant to suggest himself as a kind of Dante, wandering through this hell with his Virgil.

Martyrdom of the Ten Thousand, 1508

St. Anne with the Virgin and Child, 1519

In the paintings of his later years, Dürer produced few of the large narratives that had occupied him earlier. He shifted to a simple, uncluttered style that focused attention on expressive figure groups and powerful single portraits. In the tender scene above, for example, an immediacy and warmth is evident. Here, the youthful Madonna prays silently for her sleeping Child, as the protective St. Anne watches over them. Dürer's wife Agnes may have served as the model for St. Anne.

Dürer's half-length portrait of St. Jerome at right movingly reflects the saint's renowned gifts of scholarship and contemplation. The picture, painted in Antwerp, became a model for Netherlandish artists, many of whom copied it. Dürer's combination of still life, harmonious color and precise portraiture—the artist had hired a 93-year-old man to pose as St. Jerome—reached a climax in this work, his last religious painting before his crowning masterwork, *The Four Apostles (page 156).*

St. Jerome, 1521

1500

Albertus Durerus Noricus
ipsum me proprijs sic effin-
gebam coloribus ætatis
anno XXVIII.

V

The Shop with
the Open Doors

In 1500, two years after painting himself as a fashionable aristocrat, Dürer produced another self-portrait that showed him in a very different guise *(opposite)*. The bearded face is grave, and fringed by carefully arranged shoulder-length hair; the somewhat slanting eyes of the earlier portrait have been enlarged; a symmetry of features has been supplied that Dürer never actually possessed. The picture clearly reflects the traditional Northern European concept of what Christ Himself looked like.

Dürer's idealization of his features to conform to those of the Saviour was a deliberate act, in the opinion of the eminent art historian Erwin Panofsky, and one that was further underscored by the rigidly frontal pose of the half-length figure, and by the position of the right hand, almost as if in blessing. But, as Panofsky points out, Dürer would scarcely have entertained the blasphemous notion of himself as a reincarnated Son of Man. What he undoubtedly did believe in was the idea that every Christian was an imitator of Christ and might be so portrayed. For Dürer, this would be even more true in the case of the artist, whose creative power was derived from God and whose art might be considered to share God's act of creation. "Fervent and severe," was the way Dürer saw himself.

Whatever the varied impulses that stirred Dürer to paint his idealized self-portrait—the last he ever executed in oil—his chief aim was to leave to posterity a permanent image of himself as a universal artist. Aside from the element of vanity that may have entered into his considerations, he was an instinctive recorder, pictorially no less than in the meticulous detailing of his family life. Ironically, the self-portrait of 1500 did more than preserve his image; it helped foster the popular misconception of him as a Christlike master, aloof, awe-inspiring, impossible to know intimately.

A more accurate—and considerably more human—impression of Dürer emerges from two drawings made in the next decade, when he was in his thirties. The first, a pen-and-brush sketch of himself naked, is one that he made about 1503 when he was recovering from some illness. Here, with his hair bound back in a net, his beard crimped, his

The most celebrated of Dürer's many self-portraits is this painting, made when he was 29 and renowned throughout Europe. Frankly idealized into a Christlike image, it may have been meant by Dürer to remind viewers that an artist's creative spirit is God-given.

Self-Portrait, 1500

body wasted, he is neither the universal artist nor the man of sorrows, but a melancholy and somewhat petulant individual. A quick sketch that he sent to his physician about 1510, requesting some medical advice by letter, shows him again nude and pointing to an encircled area on his left side. "Where the yellow spot is," he wrote at the top of the paper, "and where my finger points, there is the pain"—an indication that he may have been suffering from some disease of the spleen. Once more he is wearing his unbound hair shoulder-length and has a mustache and a pointed beard, and it may be that because of the haste with which it was executed, this drawing is the closest likeness that we have of him in his middle years.

Dürer made this nude self-portrait to enable a physician whom he could not visit to diagnose a pain that he felt. The artist noted that he was pointing to the spot where it hurt. From the location of the pain and the description of his physical condition in notes and letters, doctors today believe Dürer was suffering from a disorder of the spleen; the discomfort he complained of may have been a warning of the illness that eventually killed him.

The period just after 1500 was a time of both triumph and trial for Dürer, a time in which his fame grew and his art flourished in the midst of personal and public turmoil. The prophets of doom had been proved wrong when 1500 came and went without the end of the world, but there were troubles enough even so. Outbreaks of the plague and visitations of the fearsome phenomenon of the blood rain were recurring yearly. The times themselves seemed to be raining blood. In 1502 the Margrave of Brandenburg, asserting one of the perennial Hohenzollern claims to land outside Nuremberg's walls, attacked the city; fighting at his side was one of Germany's wolf-knights—so known because of their ferocity—Götz von Berlichingen, Götz of the Iron Fist, the scourge of wealthy traveling merchants.

The Nurembergers managed to stand off margrave and wolf-knight, but the next year the city became embroiled in another war, this one between claimants to the dukedom of Bavaria. For its help to the winner, Nuremberg was allowed to keep all the nearby towns it had taken, and thus came to be the largest landholder of all the free cities of the Empire. But the price of victory was an increase in the taxes it had to pay to the Emperor, and in the small wars it had to wage to retain its new territory.

Dürer's own affairs were in a troubled state. Poor health dogged him. He had not yet begun to reap the full rewards of renown, and financial difficulties forced him to borrow from his friend Pirckheimer. In 1502, after a long period of debility, his father died. To Dürer's great sorrow he himself happened to be absent from the room at the moment of death. Recording his loss, he vowed never to forsake his mother, in a curious passage which noted that his father "was ever wont to praise her highly to me, saying what a good wife she was." Dürer's grief seems to have shaken him profoundly. "The merciful God help me also to a happy end!" he wrote. He suffered continually from fits of depression, and from tormenting dreams.

His appetite for work was nevertheless unimpaired. With the widespread distribution of his woodcuts—the *Apocalypse* series and the early sheets of *The Large Passion*—Dürer found himself recognized beyond any question as the leading German artist. Pupils began flocking to him: young men like Hans Suess from Kulmbach, Hans Schäufelein (the "little shovel," who signed his drawings with that rebus) from Swabia and Hans Baldung Grien from Strasbourg. The shop with the open doors was an increasingly busy one. Besides the usual painting and printmaking, Dürer and his assistants collaborated with goldsmiths and glass painters, preparing designs for jewelry, scabbards, chalices, goblets. They also illustrated books, among them several volumes of the Latin poems of Germany's laureate, the Nuremberger Conrad Celtes. Dürer himself drew the frontispiece for the *Quattuor Libri Amorum (The Four Books of Love),* the poem in imitation of Ovid that Celtes considered his masterpiece.

In his woodcuts, Dürer turned from the tumultuous visions of the *Apocalypse* and the tense drama of *The Large Passion* to homely narrative, in a new series—20 scenes in all—on *The Life of the Virgin.* A number of legendary stories about the Virgin, beginning with an account of her parents, Joachim and St. Anne, had become popular with the rise of the cult of Mary in the later Middle Ages. Dürer must have seen them dramatized many times in the Passion Plays given during Holy Week in front of the Church of Our Lady. In his captivating woodcuts—they are smaller than his previous woodcuts, about 11½ by 8½ inches, but still quite large for woodcuts—he retold the story of Mary with warmth and tenderness, as if it had just happened yesterday, using for his models the ordinary people he saw on the streets of Nuremberg. There are even moments of fun, as in the *Sojourn of the Holy Family in Egypt (page 107),* where Mary, with the Child in a cradle beside her, winds flax on her spindle, while Joseph in a carpenter's apron carves a block of wood with his adz; and playful little angels—one of them in a straw hat—gather up the chips and shavings and put them in a wicker basket.

The *Apocalypse* woodcuts and those of *The Large Passion* could have served as reliefs for some great carved German altar. But in *The Life of the Virgin* Dürer has moved from relief to depth. Perspective has become much more integral. Engrossed now in the problem of space, Dürer has made his figures move easily in the third dimension.

His *Life of the Virgin* series coincided with his growing concern for geometric form. In these pictures his careful work with ruler and compass is obvious. So is his continuing fascination with the Platonic notion of the ideal human figure—a figure to be drawn not from life, with its adventitious variation of bodies, but from some pure and unalterable mathematical formula such as one might have taken from Euclid or from the Roman architect Vitruvius. Fifteen hundred years earlier, Vitruvius had evolved a set of dimensions for the ideal human form: the length of the foot—from the heel to the tip of the extended big toe —should be a seventh of the height from the heel to the top of the head; the length of the face should be a tenth of the total height; the measurement from the top of the head to the chin should be an eighth of the total height; from the fingertips to the curve of the elbow, a quarter; and so on. Something of this the Italians before Dürer's time had rediscovered and redefined. All of it he determined to recapture.

Evidence of his attempts to reduce the human form to a theorem survives in a number of sketches, some of them curiously cubistic. In preliminary studies of Adam and Eve that Dürer made for his engraving of

Dürer produced hundreds of sketches like the ones above in his tireless quest for some mathematical principles that would enable him to draw the human figure with all its parts harmoniously related. Here he visualizes the head as an assembly of geometric planes.

1504, *The Fall of Man* (*pages 108-109*), he went to considerable pains to achieve a geometrical construction of the two beings he saw as the ideal man and woman. Yet in spite of the forest setting and the charm of the grouped animals—the rabbit, the ox, the elk, the parrot, the cat watching the mouse, the mountain goat on a distant crag—Dürer's figures of Adam and Eve are cold in their classicism, as if the measuring mind had checked the creating hand.

During these early years of the new century Dürer undertook relatively little formal oil painting. For his august patron Frederick the Wise he executed two more altarpieces, one of them an *Adoration of the Magi* (*pages 76-77*), in which the Virgin's face is seen in profile, wistful, half-smiling, half-wondering. He produced another altarpiece, a *Nativity*, since known as the Paumgärtner Altar, for the wealthy Nuremberg family that commissioned it. In the conventional form of a triptych, it is remarkable both for its use of central perspective and for the singular clarity of the blue sky above the Franconian meadow background. But perhaps his most striking work in oil from this period is an *Ecce Homo*, a marvelous small painting—only 11¾ by 7½ inches—that expresses in miniature the somber starkness of Grünewald's Isenheim altarpiece. Dürer's scourged and bloody Man of Sorrows leans against a sarcophagus, the crown of thorns pressed down on His head. With whip and rod resting on His knee, His hand against His face, He stares out at the world with great grieving eyes. In the tragic tortured body is reflected much of Dürer's own mood, and much of the harsh reality of the life around him.

He reverted to the themes of suffering and death, with equally powerful results, when he began experimenting for the first time with the broader line and blunter effect of charcoal. In one such drawing, the *Head of the Dead Christ,* the Saviour's features are foreshortened, as if one were looking down at Him from the foot of a bier. One sees nothing

During an outbreak of plague which took a heavy toll in 1505, Dürer made one of his most haunting charcoal sketches. It shows the crowned figure of King Death and the Latin words *Memento Mei* (Remember Me), Death's chill reminder to the living. Clutching a murderous scythe in his left hand, he leans forward to grip with his other hand the mane of his steed. The bell hanging from the animal's neck symbolizes the death knell, which tolled daily in Dürer's time as corpses were carted away for burial.

but the thorn-crowned head. The eyes are closed in agony, the mouth dropped open to show the tongue and teeth, the death sweat damp on His face. In another charcoal drawing, Dürer depicted Death itself, a crowned skeleton mounted on a bent and bony nag, hunched forward with clutched scythe like a commander-in-chief poised before battle. Death the Conqueror, ready to spur forward, surveys the plague-stricken countryside. On this quick but masterly sketch, one of the most effective he was ever to make, Dürer inscribed Death's warning to man, "Memento Mei"—remember me.

By a careful culling of Dürer's works it is easy to show how they reflect the anguish of the times. Yet during these same years he made his plant and animal studies—*The Great Piece of Turf, Columbine, Turk's Cap,* the *Parrot,* the *Young Hare,* the two engravings of horses—that so serenely reflect the glory of nature and the wonder of the God-created world as seen in all its creatures. The watercolor of the crouching hare that he kept in his studio at least long enough to paint—one can see the window bars reflected in the pupils of its eyes—is the most vital of his animal creations *(page 75).* With ears alert for any danger, whiskers twitching, the hare is ready to bound away at the least sign. The very texture of the fur is patterned to each hair, so lifelike that one could reach out to stroke it.

Dürer's meticulous rendering of individual hairs was, in fact, one of the skills that Giovanni Bellini himself most admired. In his memoir of Dürer, Joachim Camerarius told of an exchange between the two artists in the course of some shop talk in Venice about their respective techniques. As Camerarius reported it, Bellini asked Dürer to make him a present of one of the brushes with which he drew hairs. "Dürer at once produced several," Camerarius went on, "just like other brushes, and, in fact, of the kind Bellini himself used, and told him to choose those he liked best, or to take them all if he would. But Bellini, thinking he was misunderstood, said: 'No, I don't mean these but the ones with which you draw several hairs with one stroke; they must be rather spread out and more divided, otherwise in a long sweep such regularity of curvature and distance could not be preserved.' 'I use no other than these,' says Albrecht, 'and to prove it, you may watch me.' Then, taking up one of the same brushes, he drew some very long wavy tresses, such as women generally wear, in the most regular order and symmetry."

Bellini's astonishment was such, Camerarius concluded, that he "afterwards confessed to many that no human being could have convinced him by report of the truth of that which he had seen with his own eyes."

Dürer was soon to see Bellini again. In 1505 the plague once more scourged Nuremberg and the carts loaded with bodies rumbled through the streets. Those who could fled the city, the patricians as usual being the first to go. In the late summer Dürer left for Venice, leaving his wife behind and his assistants in charge of his shop. Escaping the plague was one reason for his decision. But he was also concerned with practical business matters—not only with potential sales but with protecting himself against the widespread piracy of his prints by Marcantonio Raimondi and other Italian engravers. Although he had to borrow from

Pirckheimer to make the journey, this time he traveled like a gentleman, with horses and a quantity of baggage that included a box of prints and six small paintings he planned to sell. No longer was he the unknown journeyman of 11 years before, making his way over the Brenner Pass; his reputation had now preceded him.

He traveled by way of Augsburg, staying for several weeks with a friend of Pirckheimer's who put him in touch with the gifted humanist Conrad Peutinger. Augsburg was the home of the Fuggers, that fabulously rich banking family whose gold could seat archbishops and other high-ranking prelates and swing the balance in the election of emperors. Through Peutinger Dürer was introduced to the Fuggers, and since they were the leaders of the German colony in Venice, it may be that even before Dürer arrived in that city he had received the informal promise of a commission that would in time make him the envy of the Italian studios.

The city's German center, the Fondaco dei Tedeschi, had burned down that spring and was being rebuilt, under the sponsorship of the Fuggers, by the renowned architect Jerome of Augsburg. Since the Venetian Senate had refused to allow the Germans any marble for the façade, the reconstruction posed certain difficulties, but Jerome had solved them by employing the brilliant young Venetian artist Giorgione to decorate the façade with frescoes. At the same time that they reconstituted the Fondaco, the Fuggers planned to donate the lion's share of the funds for a new altarpiece for the German colony's church, San Bartolommeo. Shortly after his arrival in Venice Dürer was given the contract for this picture, *The Feast of the Rose Garlands (pages 80-81),* which he agreed to complete within five months for a fee of 110 florins —an amount difficult to value by today's price scale, but worth in metal about 3,600 gold dollars. He lodged at Peter Pander's Inn, the leading hostelry for Germans and close to San Bartolommeo. Ten surviving letters from those he wrote to Pirckheimer have preserved the details of his daily life, his work, his pleasures, his problems, his rivalries and his associations.

As he was very well aware, Dürer in his monumental *Feast of the Rose Garlands* was challenging the Italians on their own ground. With careful confidence he made his preliminary sketches, determined, he reported to Pirckheimer, "to silence those who said that I was good as an engraver but did not know how to handle the colors in painting." Earlier pictures on the same theme—the Virgin and Child and St. Dominic, who was traditionally the founder of the popular devotion of the rosary—had hardened into a symbolic pattern. But Dürer—as he had done with his *Apocalypse* woodcuts—gave this pattern a new and overwhelming life. In his painting, the Virgin and Child distribute their rose garlands in a spring landscape at the foot of the Alps, with St. Dominic helping them in the background. Like Giovanni Bellini, Dürer had placed his Virgin under a rich canopy. Cherubs hold a crown over her head, while all Christendom gathers in unity at her feet to receive the blessing of the rosary in the form of the garlands. To her right the reigning pope, Julius II, kneels in a golden cope with

A painting of the Virgin and Child by Giovanni Bellini radiates a noble serenity and sweetness. Bellini, whom Dürer considered the greatest living Italian painter, was a pioneer in mastering the secrets of oil painting, which had been introduced in Venice from the North in the 1470s.

his triple crown beside him. Opposite him the hawk-nosed Emperor Maximilian extends his slender hands while the Virgin places a rose crown on his head. The patriarch of Venice kneels beside the Pope, and in the background under a tree Dürer has painted himself and, nearby, the architect Jerome. Today the picture is in such a damaged state that the remaining worshipers cannot be accurately determined, although some of them have been tentatively identified as members of the Fugger family and one as Conrad Peutinger.

As his work on *The Feast of the Rose Garlands* progressed, as the quality of his accomplishment became manifest, Dürer found himself faced with the growing jealousy of his Venetian colleagues, who began to sneer at the bearded man from the North. Some of them, he was informed, were even ready to poison him. "Amongst the Italians I have many good friends who warn me not to eat and drink with their painters," he wrote Pirckheimer. "Many of them are my enemies, and they copy my work in the churches and wherever they can find it; and then they revile it and say that the style is not antique and so not good. But Giovanni Bellini has highly praised me before many nobles. He wanted to have something of mine, and himself came to me and asked me to paint him something and he would pay well for it. And all men tell me what an upright man he is, so that I am very friendly with him. He is very old, but still the best painter of them all."

In their hostility the Venetian painters managed to have Dürer brought three times before the city's magistrates—on precisely what charges is not known—and he was forced as a foreigner to pay four florins to their school. But, as he told his friend, the nobles were friendly even if the painters were not. And for all the press of work and the professional hostility he encountered, Dürer managed to enjoy himself in Venice, even briefly taking dancing lessons at a school. "No one could get me to go there again," he wrote. "To learn dancing I should have had to pay away all that I have earned, and at the end I should have known nothing about it."

Dürer's letters are a lighthearted mixture of affection, badinage, gossip and accounts of his work. He mentions the French cape and the Italian coat he has bought, the gray hair he has found on his head, and the difficulties he has encountered in fulfilling Pirckheimer's orders for pearls, an emerald ring, a sapphire ring, Greek books and other sundries; he joshes Pirckheimer about the ladies in his life. He begs his friend to lend his mother money if she needs it and to keep an eye on his wayward 15-year-old brother Hanns, and he warns him archly not to make love to Agnes Dürer, as "a ponderous fellow like you would be the death of her."

"How I wish you were here at Venice!" he writes. "There are so many pleasant men among the Italians who seek my company more and more every day—which is very pleasing—men of sense and knowledge, good lute-players and pipers, judges of painting; men of much noble sentiment and honest virtue, and they show me much honor and friendship. On the other hand there are also amongst them some of the most false, lying, thievish rascals; I should never have believed that such

It is probable that while in Italy Dürer had the opportunity to inspect some of Leonardo da Vinci's work. Leonardo's masterly characterizations of human features, including this study of five grotesque heads, may have influenced the German artist's painting *Christ among the Doctors* (page 82).

were living in the world. If one did not know them, one would think them the nicest men the earth could show. For my own part I cannot help laughing at them whenever they talk to me. They know that their knavery is no secret, but they don't mind."

Dürer had planned to finish *The Feast of the Rose Garlands* in May; he did not manage to complete it until August. He had, he told Pirckheimer, with an artist's irritability, received "much praise but little profit," and he complained that he could have earned much more money working on other projects. Nevertheless, as the picture reached its completion, it was recognized as a masterpiece, and even the jealous Italians accepted Dürer's own evaluation that "there is no better Madonna picture in the land than mine. All the painters," he wrote Pirckheimer in triumph, "say that they have never seen a nobler, more charming painting, and so forth." Venetians flocked to his studio to see the new marvel, their visits culminating in the arrival of the two arch-connoisseurs of the city, the Doge himself, Leonardo Loredano, and the humanist Cardinal of St. Mark's, Domenico Grimani. So impressed was Venice with the Northerner's genius that the Senate offered him an annual pension of 200 ducats to become a permanent resident of the city.

Apparently, though, Dürer never seriously considered settling in Italy. To Pirckheimer, writing to ask when he planned to return, he replied in the middle of October: "I shall have finished here in ten days; after that I should like to ride to Bologna to learn the secrets of the art of perspective, which a man is willing to teach me. I should stay there eight or ten days and then return to Venice. After that I shall come with the next messenger. How I shall freeze after this sun! Here I am a gentleman, at home a nobody."

The man willing to teach him may have been Fra Luca Pacioli—a pupil of Piero della Francesca's and a friend of Leonardo da Vinci's—who had written treatises on perspective, although there is some question as to whether Pacioli was in Bologna at the time. Whatever practical progress he had made in perspective drawing, Dürer was increasingly preoccupied with its theory, as well as with the theories of proportion and harmony that Jacopo de' Barbari had long ago hinted at, with the quest for a mathematical formula for beauty—although in the end Dürer would finally have to admit: "What beauty is I do not know. Nobody knows it except God."

The quest that brought him to the university city at the foot of the Apennines turned out to be a personal triumph. His fellow Nuremberger, Christopher Scheurl, already in Bologna to receive his doctorate of laws, organized a celebration in his honor. The city's artists arranged a banquet for "the new Apelles," as they called him, in humanist fashion, after the Greek painter of the time of Alexander the Great. Fervently they proclaimed that he was the best painter in the world, and that they "would die the happier for having seen Dürer for whom we have yearned for so long."

Dürer returned to Venice by way of Padua and Mantua, partly to pay his respects to the master he so admired, the aged Mantegna. But when he reached Mantua he learned that Mantegna had died several months earlier; according to Camerarius' memoir, Dürer would later describe his receipt of this news as "the saddest event" of his life. In spite of his promise to Pirckheimer, he remained in Venice until the early weeks of 1507, complaining even then that he had refused work that would have brought him more than 2,000 ducats.

The six oil paintings that Dürer had brought with him to Venice he sold or bartered soon after his arrival. In those early weeks he had also painted the delicate half-length *Portrait of a Young Girl (in Milanese Dress) (page 78)*, a wistfully smiling charmer with golden hair and dark eyes and a low-cut dress of gold brocade tied by a pair of velvet bows, only one of which he completed. He painted several other portraits after he finished *The Feast of the Rose Garlands,* one of them of the stately auburn-haired wife of a German merchant *(page 79)*; at one time this work was erroneously thought to represent Agnes Dürer, since he had woven the initials "A D" on her bodice. With its emphasis on light and shade rather than line, the portrait shows an unaccustomed mellowness of style that echoes, if faintly, the work of Leonardo da Vinci. There is much more of Leonardo in the *Christ among the Doctors (page 82)* that Dürer, as he proudly inscribed on its surface, painted in five days. A radiant boy stands in the midst of six old men, their faces distorted with spite and envy as they argue with him, gesturing with their fingers in the Italian manner. Such grotesque heads Dürer had seen in Leonardo's *Treatise on Human Proportions,* and the manner of crowding the old men together as half-length figures to hide the background was another device of Leonardo's that he adopted. This picture, this contrast between the radiance of youth and the hideousness of old age, was—as he wrote Pirckheimer—like nothing he had ever done before.

Finally he ended his stay in Venice and turned homeward. Financially as well as artistically he could consider the sojourn a success. He had earned enough to repay the large sums he had borrowed from Pirckheimer, and he still had sufficient money left to redeem the mortgage on his father's house and later to buy a large corner house—afterwards to be known as the Dürer House, and still standing today—in the Zistelgasse near the Tiergärtner Gate. In the precise notebook that he kept on his domestic affairs, he recorded his possessions and his financial state:

"The following is my property, which I have with difficulty acquired by the labor of my hand, for I have had no opportunity of great gain. I have moreover suffered much loss by lending what was not repaid to me, and by apprentices who never paid their fees; and one died in Rome, whereby I lost my wares. In the thirteenth year of my marriage I have paid great debts with what I earned in Venice. I possess fairly good household furniture, good clothes, some good pewter table ware, good tools and materials for my work, bedding, chests and cupboards and paints worth more than 100 Rhenish gulden."

For the gabled building in the Zistelgasse with its roof platform that had formerly belonged to the astronomer Bernhard Walther, a pupil of Regiomontanus, he paid 550 gulden, half in cash and the rest through a mortgage. In 1509 he and his wife and his mother moved into the new house where he would live the rest of his life.

One of Nuremberg's most impressive houses, shown in this photograph, was Dürer's home from 1509 until his death in 1528. Situated in an old quarter of the city, it fronts on a street now renamed Albrecht-Dürer-Strasse. Although a bomb tore out a large portion of the building during World War II, it has since been restored as a Dürer museum. On exhibit in the 12 rooms are reproductions of many Dürer works and a few original prints.

Dürer's fame became international when thousands of his brilliant woodcuts, printed inexpensively from carved wooden blocks like the one at right, flooded across Europe and were eagerly bought by rich and poor alike. He was the first great genius of mass communications, the first to master both woodcuts and engravings as well as etchings and dry points, and his emerging skill coincided perfectly with the development of cheap paper and improved printing equipment.

Dürer's first major success in the graphic arts, hailed both in his native Germany and elsewhere, was *The Apocalypse,* published in 1498, a series of 15 woodcuts illustrating the Revelation of St. John that heralded the end of the world. Dürer followed this with a series known as *The Large Passion,* on the last days, Death and Resurrection of Christ, and with another set of woodcuts depicting the life of the Virgin.

Drawing on many of the same rich Biblical sources that had inspired his woodcuts, Dürer's engravings also reflect the religious fervor of the time. Most of the engravings, however, were aimed at a much smaller and more sophisticated audience and were filled with obscure symbols that have fascinated scholars for centuries. But even in these sometimes perplexing works, Dürer blended intense spirituality with painstaking attention to nature. It is these qualities in his graphic work that made him the most popular artist of his day.

The Triumph of Line

Carved by the Master

Shown at the right is an irreplaceable art treasure—a wood block that was probably cut by Dürer himself. Unusual in its day because it was carved by the artist rather than by a craftsman following the artist's design, the block is reproduced at slightly less than its actual size and shows (in reverse) Samson killing a lion with his bare hands. (Above, reduced in size, is a print from the wood block.) Light areas on the block show where wood has been gouged away; the dark lines are the ridges left to receive the ink. Dürer's genius lay in carving lines—as in the lion's mane—that do more than simply outline a form; they swell and taper expressively to give convincing life to each element in the design.

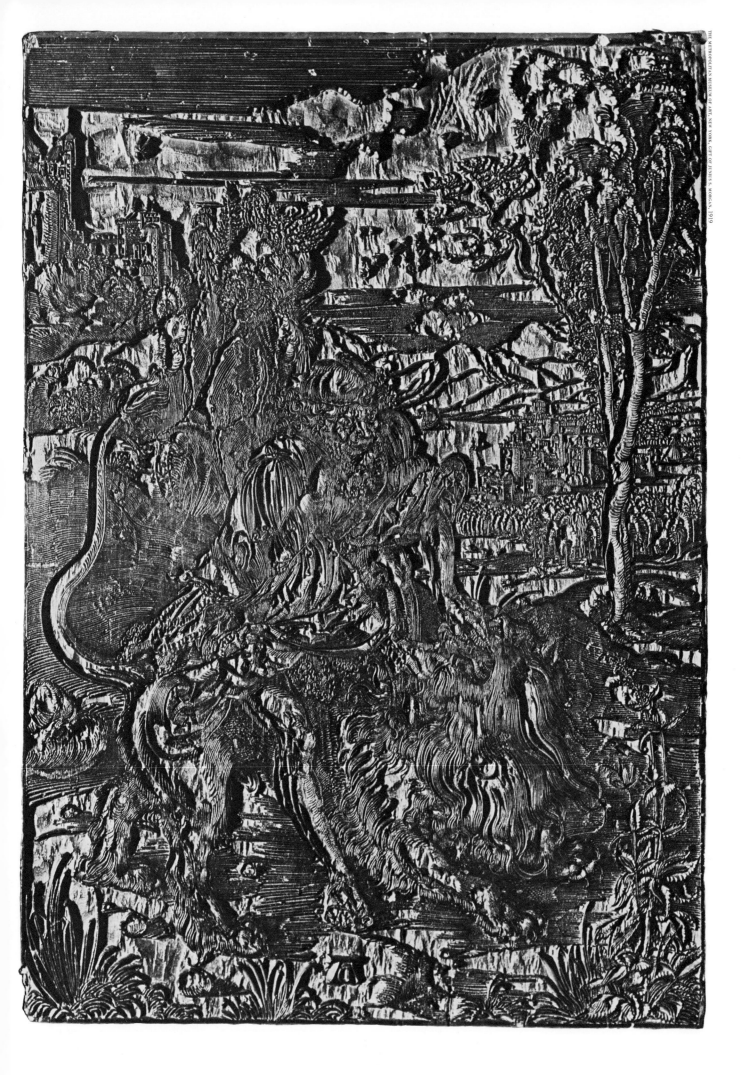

The Apocalypse

Dürer's "Apocalypse" series begins with this woodcut showing the first of St. John's many prophetic visions described in his "Revelation." Here, God appears to the saint, holding the Book of Doom, which tells of an imminent cosmic holocaust that will consume all evil. Seven magnificent candlesticks light the sky, as the saint kneels reverently before the Lord.

The fourth print of the series is one of Dürer's best-known woodcuts. In it, the Four Horsemen —representing, from left to right, Death, Famine, Pestilence and War—ride rampant over the earth. Under the eyes of an angel, the three powerful horses and riders trample men and women, while Death's bony nag treads upon a bishop falling into the gaping jaws of the Dragon of Hell.

Many of the disasters climaxing the Apocalypse are crowded into this single woodcut, seventh in the series. As God watches and angels trumpet the approach of calamity, a pair of giant hands plunge a mountain into the sea, a star falls, ships founder and fires and locusts ravage the land. Near the center, Dürer showed an eagle screeching the German words "Woe, woe, woe."

In the final woodcut of the series, evil is overcome. An angel with a key imprisons a monstrous Satan in a pit that is fitted with a stout and intricately locking lid. Another angel shows St. John the way to the New Jerusalem, where the righteous will gather to live in peace. For the architecture of the holy city, Dürer based his buildings largely on the styles of his own Nuremberg.

Passio domini nostri Jesu.ex hierony

mo Paduano.Dominico Mancino.Sedulio.et Baptista Mantuano.per fratrem Chelidonium colle
cta.cum figuris Alberti Dureri
Norici Pictoris.

Has ego crudeles homo pro te perfero plagas

Atqȝ meo morbos sanguine curo tuos.

Vulneribusqȝ meis tua vulnera.morteqȝ mortem

Tollo deus:pro te plasmate factus homo.

Tuqȝ ingrate mihi:pungis mea stigmata culpis

Sæpe tuis.noxa vapulo sæpe tua.

Sat fuerit.me tanta olim tormenta sub hoste

Iudæo passum:nunc sit amice quies.

The Large Passion

In 1511 Dürer published a series depicting the later life of Christ. The 12 woodcuts, some
of which had earlier been issued singly, were called "The Large Passion" because of the size of
the prints—11 by 15 inches. The title page, above, bears Dürer's name in Latin, a poem
berating man for his sins, and an illustration showing a Roman soldier mocking Christ.

This woodcut from "The Large Passion," showing Christ's descent into Limbo after His Crucifixion, almost achieves the effect of an engraving in its subtle shadings. Behind Christ stand Adam (holding the Cross), Eve and others under His protection. In the grotesque beasts at right Dürer has enriched the traditional medieval German concept of Hell's denizens.

EPITOME IN DIVAE PARTHENICES MARI AE HISTORIAM AB ALBERTO DVRERO NORICO PER FIGVRAS DIGES TAM CVM VERSIBVS ANNE XIS CHELIDONII

Quisquis fortunæ correptus turbine.perfers
Quam tibi iacturam fata sinistra ferunt.
Aut animæ delicta gemis.Phlegethontis & ignes
Anxius æternos corde tremente paues.
Quisquis & vrgeris iam iam decedere vita
Alterius:migrans:nescius hospitij.
Huc ades:auxilium:pete:continuoq; rogabo
Pro te:quem paui lacte:tuliq; sinu.
Ille deus rerum mihi subdidit astra:deosq;
Flectitur ille meis O homo supplicijs.

The Life of the Virgin

106

*In the same year that Dürer published "The Large Passion," he brought out his
"Life of the Virgin," 20 woodcuts introduced by this exquisite title page. Here Mary is depicted
both as a nursing mother and as a divine being framed by the crescent moon, the stars and a burst of
heavenly light. As in "The Large Passion," a Latin verse accompanied each woodcut.*

Dürer turns away from mighty spiritual themes in this gentle, domestic scene showing the
Holy Family in Egypt during their exile from Jerusalem. As God watches benignly
from above, a matronly Mary spins while rocking the Infant and the carpenter Joseph is
assisted in his work by a group of beguiling cherubs who collect the scattered wood chips for him.

The Progress of an Engraving

While Dürer was engraving his *Fall of Man* in 1504 —it is shown in its finished form at right—he "pulled" the trial proofs reproduced above, which offer a rare opportunity to see two early stages, called "states" by engravers, of a masterpiece in the making. They also reveal how skillfully he used the subtle definitions and delicate shadings of the engraving technique—qualities that infuse all the Dürer engravings on the following pages.

Using a sharp steel tool called a burin, the artist first lightly incised the outlines of his entire composition on a smooth copper plate. The sketchy white areas in the proofs above show this light drawing. In the proof at left, Dürer has fully incised Adam's right leg and such background details as the parrot, the serpent and the Trees of Life and Knowledge. In the later proof at right, the artist has filled in Adam's left leg and part of the ground at his feet. Such proofs enabled Dürer to check his effects periodically, since it was difficult for the artist, as it is for all engravers, to determine in advance exactly how the lines cut into the plate will transfer the ink to paper.

108

The Fall of Man

In his engraving of Adam and Eve about to take the Forbidden Fruit, Dürer has mixed symbolism and realism to great effect. The elk, rabbit, cat and ox represent the evil humors of melancholy, sensuality, cruelty and sluggishness. At the same time Dürer has achieved in the two beautifully rendered figures one of his finest expressions of a lifelong search for ideal human proportions.

The Prodigal Son

One of Dürer's earliest engravings illustrates the moment in the parable of the Prodigal Son
when the youth, having squandered his fortune, falls to his knees among the swine and resolves
to return home to ask his father's forgiveness. Although the work shows that Dürer had not yet found
an ideal of human proportion, his rendering of the farmyard scene is faultless.

The Sea Monster

One of the artist's most enigmatic engravings shows an exotically coifed maiden being abducted by a bizarre sea creature, while on the shore a man waves his arms in alarm. This curiously dreamlike scene, in which the woman appears paradoxically unruffled as her captor swims off with her, may have been based on widely believed 15th Century reports of sea monsters kidnapping women bathers.

St. Eustace

In his charming engraving of St. Eustace, the legendary Roman soldier who became a Christian after witnessing the miracle of a stag bearing a Crucifix, Dürer displayed his skill in recording the natural world. The accuracy of his observation is apparent everywhere: in the animals, in the varied foliage, even in the almost invisible flock of birds circling the distant castle.

Nemesis   *In this engraving the ponderous, sinister figure of Nemesis, the goddess of retribution, hovers over the earth, controlling the fortunes of those below. In one hand she holds a bridle and bit, symbols of punishment; in the other, a chalice, a symbol of reward. The landscape beneath her, a Tyrolean valley, reveals once more Dürer's attention to natural and architectural detail.*

Knight, Death and Devil

In an allegory on the strength of the true Christian faith, Dürer depicted a steadfast knight riding untroubled past the swine-snouted figure of the Devil, and Death, who waves an hourglass symbolizing the shortness of life. Dürer's knight, following St. Paul's Biblical admonition to the faithful, has shielded himself from the wiles of the Devil with the "armor of God."

Melencolia I

The most complex of all Dürer's engravings, this work has long confounded scholars seeking to explain its symbolic nuances. Most agree that the brooding, winged figure represents the artistic genius despairing of inspiration. But there is little agreement about the significance of many artifacts, such as the "magic square" at the upper right, whose columns all add up to 34.

St. Jerome in His Study

Details of the life of St. Jerome, a Fourth Century Christian scholar, were well known in Dürer's day, and in this print the artist used the saint to idealize the contemplative Christian life. Legend held that Jerome befriended a lion by pulling a thorn from its paw, and Dürer has shown the animal guarding his master's peaceful study from worldly intrusions.

The Desperate Man

After completing his great engravings and still seeking new modes of expression, Dürer tried etching—a newly developed technique in which the design was incised on a metal plate with acid rather than cut by hand. This puzzling etching, apparently composed at random, was not titled by Dürer. Its name comes from the central figure, who tears his hair in a frenzy.

Imperator Caelar Diuus Maximilianus
Pius Felix Auguftus

VI

In the Emperor's Service

Dürer had clearly exaggerated when, looking forward to his return home from Venice, he described himself as "a nobody" in Nuremberg. He lived in an imposing house, was the friend of scholars and patricians, and enjoyed the patronage of the Elector Frederick. Indeed, his position in the community was recognized by his selection at Easter 1509 as a member of Nuremberg's Grand Council, a group of 200 men of wealth or noble lineage who sometimes added to their number fellow citizens who had distinguished themselves in other ways. The council, although consulted on questions of war and public policy, had no powers of real importance, since the actual government of the city rested in the hands of an inner council of 34 patricians and eight artisans. Nevertheless, to be allowed to sit in the Great Assembly Room of the Town Hall was a sign that a man was accepted as one of the leaders of the community.

Dürer's new position did not interfere with his artistic production. Settled once more in his studio, he turned to the proportion studies of his *Fall of Man* engraving as the basis for two paintings of *Adam and Eve (page 83)*. This time he shifted his emphasis from a geometrical construction to his conception of the first pair as ideal human beings. In his narrow life-sized paintings they are poised against dark backgrounds like dancers: Adam, a young Apollo with his supple brown body, his head thrown back and his mouth open, the radiancy of his loose-curled golden hair reflected in his face; Eve, of a porcelain whiteness, standing by the Tree of Life, shyly taking the apple from the serpent. Yet both figures, even as they give way to original sin, embody the pervading innocence of the newly created. For all her nakedness there is in Eve nothing of the erotic that one finds in her successors, the Eves and Venuses painted with such enticing fluency by Dürer's contemporaries Cranach and Baldung. Dürer's Adam and Eve are unique, reaching beyond the sinuosities of the Gothic and the severe classicism of Mantegna—and their freedom from any formula is the essence of their charm.

In 1507 Dürer was commissioned by the Elector Frederick to paint a *Martyrdom of the Ten Thousand (pages 84-85)*, the subject being the execution by King Shapur of Persia of 10,000 knights who had become

This woodcut by Dürer of the Holy Roman Emperor Maximilian, was based on a drawing he made a year before the monarch died. Although resplendent in his chivalric regalia, Maximilian projects a weariness of spirit, born, perhaps, of the failure of many of his grand schemes.

Maximilian I, c. 1519

converted to Christianity and preferred death to renouncing their faith. Like the similar legend of St. Ursula and the 11,000 virgins who were said to have been put to death near Cologne by the Huns in the Third Century, the story of the massacre had become extremely popular in the 15th Century. Ten years before, Dürer had represented this event in a large woodcut in which, despite the brutality of the theme, the killers and the killed bore some relation to the landscape. In the small painting for Frederick, with its more than a hundred figures, there is no such relationship. Possibly Dürer had lost interest in the subject; whatever the reason, the picture is uninspired. It is a monstrous miniature, both in conception and detail. At first glance one seems to see a Franconian summer landscape with incidental figures, on second glance a compendium of mass murder. While King Shapur in a billowing white turban supervises the slaughter, his soldiers hunt down the naked and half-robed knights through the shrubbery. Symbolic of Christ's martyrdom, some Christians are crowned with thorns, scourged, crucified; others are stoned, beheaded, transfixed with spears, hurled from cliffs.

Again, as in his more appealing *Feast of the Rose Garlands,* the artist has put himself in his own picture—standing in a black cloak in the center and holding a banner, like a safe-conduct, on which are written Dürer's name and the date, 1508. Beside him is a second spectator, possibly Pirckheimer but more probably the poet Conrad Celtes, who had died a few months before. Even if Dürer left most of the sanguinary details to his assistants, he must have found the intricacy of this picture tiresome. After working on it for a year he complained that the pre-arranged fee of 280 gulden did not pay him adequately for his time.

When Holy Roman Emperor Rudolf II bought Dürer's *Adoration of the Trinity (above)* in 1585, he left behind its magnificently carved wooden frame, which was fitted to the altar where the picture was displayed. The composite photograph above reunites the painting (now in the Kunsthistoriches Museum, Vienna) and the frame (in the Germanisches Museum, Nuremberg) exactly as Dürer intended them to be seen.

It was while working on the *Martyrdom* that Dürer met the Frankfort merchant Jacob Heller and contracted with him to paint the altarpiece for the Dominican church in Frankfort for which the "Praying Hands" drawing was a preliminary study. Heller, rich, childless and morbidly afraid of death, was anxious to perpetuate himself through charity and works of art, although his piety did not hinder him from driving a hard bargain. He agreed to pay 130 florins for the finished picture, *The Assumption and Coronation of the Virgin.* Dürer's letters to Heller, after he had begun his work, are full of complaints at the smallness of the sum. He insisted that he must have 200 florins, that left to himself he could get 300 for the finished picture, and that he would not undertake such "painstaking drudgery" again for 400. At one point he even offered to buy the picture back for the sum he had already received. Heller was not a man easily persuaded to alter the terms of a bargain, but he finally agreed to pay the 200 Dürer asked, as well as to present a piece of jewelry to Agnes and a two-florin tip to Dürer's younger brother Hanns, who had by this time joined Dürer as an assistant in his studio.

Even before Dürer finished the Heller altarpiece he had contracted to paint another one, *The Adoration of the Trinity,* for the Nuremberg metal merchant Matthias Landauer. Some years before, Landauer had founded a hostel for poor, single old men called the House of the Twelve Brothers, and now he wanted an altarpiece for its new chapel. This painting, whose frame was carved to Dürer's design by the great Nuremberg woodcarver Veit Stoss, is somewhat larger than the *Martyrdom*—about four by four-and-a-half feet—and also crowded with figures. Yet here, for all the limitations of space, Dürer has realized his basic conception of God the Father, God the Son and God the Holy Ghost surrounded by the angels, saints and men of grace who, according to the vision of St. Augustine, people the City of God.

The picture forms a multileveled unity. On the highest level of the heavens God the Father supports the cross of the crucified Christ, and the dove of the Holy Ghost flutters overhead. On the middle level, the Virgin Mary leads a multitude of female saints while John the Baptist marshals the heroes of the Old Testament, Moses, David and the prophets. On the lower level are crowded the people of this world. Beside the kneeling Pope Julius are clerics, a cardinal, nuns, and, inconspicuously, the gray-haired Landauer. Opposite them kneels a bearded emperor wearing Charlemagne's crown, with princes in purple, a king, a knight in gilded armor, men and women in the dress of Nuremberg burghers, and gnarled peasants. The quiet landscape of the earth below contains but one small solitary figure, that of the artist.

Here, in an era when popes quarreled with emperors and kings, when violence and war were everywhere, Dürer has envisioned an ideal Christian world where a purified church and state are united in their devotion to God, where noblemen, townsmen and peasants at last live in peace. He has created from the multitude of figures a graceful yet powerful composition that reveals the strength of his own hope and faith.

Despite his success with *The Adoration of the Trinity* in 1511, Dürer never again attempted the intricacies of such many-figured compositions. He once explained to his humanist friend Philip Melanchthon that "as I grew older, I realized that it was much better to insist on the genuine forms of nature, for simplicity is the greatest adornment of art."

Over the next four years he concentrated on engraving, and seemed to lose interest in oils, though he painted three incidental pictures. In 1512 he produced the small *Madonna with the Pear*—a half-length figure of the Virgin with a chubby Italianate Christ Child holding a pear —that he may have intended as a gift for Pirckheimer. That same year, at the request of the Nuremberg Council, he undertook idealized portraits of two of the greatest rulers of the Holy Roman Empire, Charlemagne and Sigismund, to decorate the room in the Town Hall where the Imperial insignia and relics were sometimes kept. It would have been hard for Dürer to refuse the Council, particularly since the portraits were intended to honor a state visit by the present Emperor, Maximilian. But after that he did not touch his oils again until 1516, when he painted a nostalgic portrait of his aged mentor, Michael Wolgemut; he would undertake no large religious paintings until his *Four Apostles* of 1526.

The year 1511 was an extraordinary one for Dürer. In that one year he published all the greatest of his woodcut series, what he called his "three large books"—*The Apocalypse, The Large Passion* and *The Life of the Virgin.* He had been working on the individual woodcuts in each of these series for years, and many of them had been printed singly, but only *The Apocalypse* had been previously issued in book form, in Ger-

The last days of Christ, a recurrent theme in late medieval art, served as the subject of several series by Dürer, including *The Engraved Passion,* published in 1513. This series—16 engravings in all—is distinctive in that it was published primarily for connoisseurs, and thus omitted the explanatory text customarily supplied for the untutored layman. The eighth engraving of the series *(above),* shows Pilate publicly challenging Christ's divinity with the Latin words *Ecce Homo* (Behold the Man). In the 12th print *(below),* Christ is lowered from the Cross.

man and Latin editions in 1498. The 1511 edition, in Latin, received a new title page. Both *The Large Passion,* with four new woodcuts done in 1510, and *The Life of the Virgin,* with three recently finished woodcuts, were now published as a group for the first time; on the page opposite each was a printed explanation in Latin verse by Dürer's friend Benedictus Chelidonius, the abbot of a Viennese monastery.

In addition to these works, Dürer also published a quarto edition, about five inches by four inches in page size, of the 37 *Small Passion* woodcuts. Though less dramatic than the others, this quarto *Passion* is the most comprehensive of all Dürer's Passion series. Intended to appeal to a wide, unlettered public, it is a clear and simple story of the Redemption, from the fall of Adam and Eve through the birth of Christ to the Crucifixion, Resurrection, Ascension and Last Judgment.

These smaller woodcuts demonstrate a significant development in Dürer's woodcut technique that occurred after his return from Venice. His earlier woodcuts had shown merely a white surface impressed by designs in black. The new effect was much more subtle; a shaded gray is the "middle" tone to which the deep shadows and bright highlights are contrasted. Dürer achieved these delicate but striking gradations by increasing the fineness of the lines—particularly the cross-hatchings—that he cut into the wood blocks. From this time on, his woodcuts show an increasing tendency to resemble engravings. In their refinement, however, they often lose the vitality of his earlier work in this medium.

In 1513 Dürer published the 16 copperplates of the so-called *Engraved Passion,* the last of his great series. It is a much more sophisticated counterpart of *The Small Passion,* modest in size but rich in detail, a work intended for connoisseurs and collectors. With it, Dürer entered his great period of engraving, which culminated in the three masterpieces, *Knight, Death, and Devil* of 1513 and *St. Jerome in his Study* and *Melencolia I* of the following year. He led up to them with an engraving in 1513 of the Sudarium—the kerchief on which appeared the imprint of Christ's anguished face after St. Veronica used it to comfort Him on His way to Calvary. In Dürer's work two young angels, poised in the outer sphere of heaven beyond space and time, hold up the kerchief; on it are fixed with almost photographic realism the Saviour's drawn features and sorrowing eyes. Here, most distinctly, Dürer has created the uniquely German conception of the countenance of Christ.

In *Knight, Death, and Devil* Dürer has presented the embodiment of Christian resolution, the knight who makes his way to his goal in defiance of Death and Hell *(page 114).* The scene is a forbidding wilderness, the Devil a swine-snouted monster with bat's wings and a single horn. Death is no longer a skeleton but a sad-eyed, decaying corpse without lips or nose, who holds up an hourglass as he swings his sorry nag athwart the path. The knight rides straight ahead, impervious, his face stern under the raised visor of his helmet. Living oak leaves are tied in his horse's bridle and tail, in contrast to the serpents intertwined on Death's head. A skull lies in the way, but he regards it as little as the salamander under his horse's hoofs. The formidable figure advancing along the abyss of life, contemptuous of lurking perils, becomes the essence of human courage. Generations have found this quality in the engraving. The anti-Christian philosopher Friedrich Nietzsche, despite his convictions, saw the knight as a "symbol of our existence."

Dürer's counterpart to the Christian knight riding indomitably through the world is the unworldly Christian scholar, St. Jerome. In the later middle ages the history of St. Jerome, the learned hermit who translated a number of books of the Bible into Latin, was an extremely popular one. Jerome had led an ascetic, pious life, much of it in a rock-hewn cell in Bethlehem, and legend had it that he had befriended a lion by pulling a thorn from its paw. Many artists drew the subject, and sophisticated ecclesiastical dignitaries liked to have themselves depicted in this other-worldly guise. Cardinal Albrecht of Brandenburg had Lucas Cranach paint him several times as the scholar-saint. Dürer, after his first crude Basel woodcut of Jerome in 1492, kept coming back to the theme. He made a large woodcut in 1511, a woodcut and a dry point the following year, and, after the publication of the great engraving, a pen drawing and an oil painting.

In the engraving *(page 116)*, Dürer has transformed Jerome's cell into a cozy room, its thick walls a fortress against the outside world. The sunlight streaming in through the round windowpanes seems to irradiate Jerome's bald head as he sits at his table, bent over his writing stand, with a small crucifix in front of him. The room, drawn in unobtrusively exact perspective, breathes a quiet warmth. In the foreground Jerome's lion, looking more like a large tomcat, sprawls drowsily beside a dog. (Dürer would not learn how to draw lions convincingly until he saw one alive in the Netherlands years later.) The saint's sandals are tucked under a bench. A cardinal's *galèro* hangs on the wall, like a gardener's hat, between an hourglass and a shelf on which are candlesticks and other domestic utensils. There are comfortable cushions on the chair and scattered on the wall bench next to odd folio volumes, and even the skull perched on the window sill manages to look benign. A huge gourd has been hung from the ceiling to dry. Here indeed is the life of contemplation with all its homely blessings.

The third great engraving, *Melencolia I*, followed the death of Dürer's mother in May 1514. He was at her bedside at the moment of death and later recorded that he "marked she saw something dreadful, for she asked for holy water, although for a long time she had not spoken. Immediately afterward she closed her eyes. I saw too how Death struck her two great strokes in the heart, and how she closed her mouth and eyes and departed with pain. I repeated prayers for her. I felt so grieved for her I cannot express it. God be merciful to her. . . . And in her death," he added, "she looked much more at peace than when she was alive." She was the person he loved most in the world, with an affection he was never able to transfer to his wife, and his dark mood after her death may well be reflected in the brooding intensity of *Melencolia I* months later. This work concluded Dürer's great period of engraving.

His artistic output in general had begun to fall off as a result of an event in 1512 that was to alter his future course. In February of that year he entered the employ of the Emperor Maximilian, who was then on a state visit to Nuremberg. Maximilian had been searching all over his realm for poets, musicians, artists, architects and historians to further various projects of self-glorification. These were limited in their imaginative scope only by the meager substance of the imperial treasury. Maximilian fancied himself variously as King Arthur and as the descendant of Hercules and of the Egyptian God Osiris. He was known as "the last of the knights" because of his romantic preoccupation with the chivalric code of earlier times. Yet for all his notions, he was a man of warmth and rare personal charm, a popular emperor, a colorful exception to the drab line of Habsburg rulers.

The Last of the Knights was tall, flaxen-haired, with blue eyes and a proud arched nose. As a daring young man he had scaled the 350-foot tower of Ulm Cathedral, the tallest spire in Europe, by means of the iron rings used to support lamps on illumination days. Boldness, coupled with lack of judgment, was characteristic of him. Enamored of tournaments and pageants, dreaming of a new crusade, he was in a way not attuned to his own age; on the other hand he was sympathetic to the humanist thinking of the day, and founded several universities in his realm.

Maximilian's mind ranged widely if superficially. Besides his archaic concern with chivalry, he prided himself on his skills in a variety of fields, from mining, ordnance, carpentry, veterinary surgery, fishing, cooking and fashion designing to jurisprudence, education, art criticism, painting, music and poetry. He studied the art of war but was unfortunate in his practice of it, engaging in ill-considered adventures out of vanity and dynastic pretension.

Whatever wealth and influence Maximilian enjoyed came through his Habsburg inheritance as Archduke of Austria, Count of Tyrol and Duke of Styria. But in his insubstantial role of Holy Roman Emperor he insisted on regarding himself primarily as a Caesar, and like Caesar he determined to be remembered by posterity in literature and art. He planned to write or to have written 130 books, although he finished only *Theuerdank,* the romanticized account of his wooing of his first wife, Mary of Burgundy. Two other books he planned were allegorical imitations of the old court epics, in which he appeared as a knight errant engaged in interminable chivalric adventures. The hundreds of woodcut illustrations for these three volumes were designed by Schäufelein, Burgkmair and some possibly by Dürer.

Maximilian also planned a giant stone memorial to decorate the Cathedral of the city of Speyer, but it was never cut; an equestrian statue that he envisaged for Augsburg was never cast. His tomb is his sole monument in stone and metal, and that was not completed until several generations after his death in 1519. Ironically, the massive sarcophagus on which his bronze likeness kneels is empty. It was built at Innsbruck, which Maximilian hoped would be his final resting place, but he died and was buried hundreds of miles away.

He did achieve the completion of at least one of his pet artistic projects. The Roman Emperors Augustus, Titus and Constantine had had arches erected in their honor under which great triumphal processions were to pass. Maximilian felt that as a Caesar he too must leave

In a merry engraving, Dürer pokes fun at a plump peasant couple kicking up their heels in a lusty country dance. Unlike some of his contemporaries, who scorned such subjects, Dürer took much pleasure in depicting common folk. "It is to be noted," he wrote, "that a sensitive, trained artist portraying a coarse, rustic figure can show more greatness and skill in humble objects than many another artist in his major work."

a triumphal arch to posterity. Since his limited budget could not stand the considerable expense of an arch of stone and mortar, he determined on an arch of paper.

The Triumphal Arch (pages 130-133) is a sectional woodcut—the largest ever made—printed from 192 separate blocks to form an assembled rectangle about 10 feet wide by 11 feet high. Johannes Stabius, the Emperor's historian, poet and astronomer, was responsible for the detailed conception. Jörg Kölderer, an Innsbruck architect, prepared the architectural framework. Dürer, with Pirckheimer as adviser in iconographical matters, acted as designer-in-chief, drawing much of the ornamental effects but leaving most of the separate scenes to his assistants.

Like the Roman triumphal arches, Maximilian's had three portals—the central Gate of Honor and Power, flanked by the Gates of Nobility and of Praise. But there any resemblance to Roman models ceased, for the Triumphal Arch soars above its three narrow portals to explode in a fantasy of turrets, domes, cupolas, round and square towers, columns and pedestals that is not Classical, Gothic or Renaissance; nor does it even look much like an arch.

Every foot of the vast surface is elaborated with some scene or design —battles that never took place, animals that never existed. Here all the paper world pays homage to Maximilian, his military exploits and his marriages, his personal accomplishments, his relatives and alleged relatives. Four Habsburg emperors on columns proclaim the glory of their descendant, as does St. Leopold, the one Habsburg saint. Roman and German emperors, from Julius Caesar to Rudolph I, pose on their pedestals, with Alphonso of Spain and Richard the Lion-Hearted thrown in for good measure. Maximilian's family tree winds its way up a façade flanked by the 108 coats of arms of the dynasty's many branches. Heralds and trumpeters stand on the cornices, apes squat on the steps, griffins stick out their tongues, goats perch along the ledges, Pans cavort. In this monstrous picture puzzle every creature and object has its symbolic meaning. It is allegory gone mad. Overlooking it all, just under the crowning central cupola with its phoenix-crest, stands Maximilian in his coronation robes, surveying his creation.

For all the indiscriminate profusion of *The Triumphal Arch,* many of the individual decorations are beautifully executed. The painter Albrecht Altdorfer, Dürer's contemporary, made 10 woodcuts for the two outer towers, reflecting the Emperor's self-image by showing him as an architect, as a jousting knight in full armor, as a preacher of a crusade, and as a master in seven languages.

To this marvel of misplaced ingenuity Dürer devoted three unpaid years. One can see his touch in some of the floral festoons, the insignia, and the fabulous animals *(pages 132-133).* Maximilian, always short of funds, first tried to recompense him by requesting the Nuremberg Council to free their fellow citizen from all municipal taxes. Although the councilors could not directly refuse the Emperor, they privately sent several of their members to Dürer in protest. To keep the goodwill of his townsmen, he agreed to decline the offer of tax-free status. At last in 1515, after supervising the cutting of 92 of the wood blocks, Dürer

Dürer's artistry is generally considered to have suffered during the six years he spent on the grandiose projects of Maximilian I. These woodcuts, for example, intended for a never-published book glorifying the Emperor's chivalric deeds, lack the majestic drama of Dürer's earlier *Apocalypse* prints *(pages 100-103).* In the print above, the Emperor unseats an opponent in a joust; below, he engages another foe. The clouds, sky and landscapes of both woodcuts are perfunctory: Dürer seems to have concentrated his energy on the scuffles themselves in the manner of a combat manual.

was rewarded by the Emperor with a pension of 100 florins a year. Typically, Maximilian asked the burgomaster and council of Nuremberg to pay the sum and deduct it from their customary contribution to the imperial exchequer.

Since a triumphal arch is incomplete without its triumph, Maximilian now set his artists to work on a *Triumphal Procession,* which he himself conceived although the details were turned over to his secretary, Marx Treitz-Saurwein. The secretary gave his imagination free rein. He planned a cortege led by a nude herald on a griffin, to be followed by a horseborne litter with the "Title Tablet"; then a procession of courtiers including mimes, fools, fencers and jousters; these in turn followed by a great line of horsemen bearing the banners of the imperial provinces. In addition there were to be self-propelled cars of war, chariots with trophies, chariots with effigies of earlier emperors, and a section showing the wedding of Maximilian and Mary of Burgundy. The climax of the procession was to be Maximilian's great triumphal car.

When Maximilian died in 1519, work on the unfinished *Procession* ceased, and not until 1526 was the fragment published, by the Emperor's grandson Archduke Ferdinand. But even though only 139 of the projected 208 woodcuts had been completed, the work when published was almost 60 yards long. Of all these woodcuts, only *The Burgundian Marriage (pages 134-135),* with Maximilian and Mary standing in a six-wheeled car under a canopy held by plump cupids, was the actual work of Dürer, though others had been executed to his designs.

Before Maximilian's death, Dürer had made a preliminary watercolor sketch of *The Great Triumphal Car.* It was never included in the *Procession* for which it was intended, but the theme, as revised by Pirckheimer, became the subject of eight woodcuts that Dürer published of his own accord in 1522. These, like the Arch itself, were weighed down with allegory, to the point that even the wheels were put to use to represent Dignity, Glory, Magnificence and Honor.

In contrast to the avid ornateness of the *Arch* and the *Procession* woodcuts, Dürer's marginal designs for the *Prayer-Book of Maximilian I* are among the freest and most delightful sketches his pen ever drew. The

Prayer-Book—a compilation of psalms, hymns, prayers and excerpts from the Gospels arranged by Maximilian—was printed on vellum in Augsburg in 1513, and five copies still exist. Four are undecorated. The fifth, the Emperor's personal copy, has a profusion of colored marginal drawings by Dürer, Cranach, Burgkmair, Baldung, and possibly also Altdorfer and Hanns Dürer.

It is open to question whether this lavishly decorated volume was intended merely for the private use of the Emperor, or whether the drawings are preliminary sketches for a colored woodcut edition, possibly for the knights of Maximilian's Order of St. George. Whatever their purpose, the *Prayer-Book* decorations released all the whimsy of Dürer's imagination, so long held in check by the ponderous reins of allegory. Up and down the blank vellum his pen raced, tracing kaleidoscopic fantasies in red, olive-green and violet, creating some of the most beautiful drawings in German art. These margins are no mere catalogue, but the very profusion of life. Flowers, foliage, animal and human figures, grotesque creatures range exuberantly up and down the borders. The pages are alive with cranes, hawks, woodpeckers, ducks, flies and lizards; elephants, apes, camels, dragons; knights, burghers, beggars, doctors, saints, devils, hermits and even the American Indians whom Columbus had brought back from the New World a few decades before. Sometimes Dürer follows the text exactly, sometimes the mere mention of a word starts him off on a detour of extemporization. "Temptation" is seen as a fox playing a flute to lure a flock of chickens within his reach. Seven lusty musicians with drums and trumpets "sing unto the Lord a new song."

When Goethe for the first time saw the *Prayer-Book* illustrations in a lithograph reproduction, he felt that they were like "the peace of God which passeth all understanding." Of one drawing, showing a peasant woman with a basket of eggs, cheese and a goose balanced on her head, he wrote: "Dürer's unsurpassed masterpiece."

Two years before Maximilian died, a little-known Augustinian monk and university lecturer took a single step that was more dramatic than all of Maximilian's grandiose schemes put together. On All Hallows Eve, 1517, Martin Luther struck the spark of the Reformation when he tacked on the door of Wittenberg's Castle Church his 95 arguments against the validity of papal indulgences, then being hawked around the countryside under the auspices of the powerful prelate Albrecht of Brandenburg. Not content with being Archbishop of Magdeburg, Albrecht had decided that he also wanted the archbishopric of Mainz, and in 1514 the Vatican gave him the appointment, on the promise of a payment of 24,000 ducats. Albrecht borrowed part of this huge sum from the banking family of the Fuggers. Then, to help him get out of debt, the elegant Medici Pope, Leo X, granted Albrecht the wholesale privilege of selling indulgences in his territories for eight years. It was a good bargain for both sides. Half the money would go to repay the Fuggers, the rest to Rome for the building of St. Peter's. Albrecht entrusted the retailing of these papal indulgences to a shrewd Dominican preacher, Johann Tetzel. The indulgences he offered for sale remitted all sins upon confession, and subscribers were guaranteed the state of innocence they had

Among Dürer's freest and most playful drawings are the 45 he contributed to Emperor Maximilian's private prayer book. The page above shows a portion of the 24th Psalm, printed in Gothic type accompanied by Dürer's fanciful notion of an American Indian. Musicians, a hermit and various bizarre creatures, decorations for another page, are shown opposite. Dürer's lighthearted illustrations, often unrelated to the text, apparently were intended not only to edify his Emperor but to lift his melancholic spirits.

One of the most powerful prelates of Dürer's time was Albrecht, Archbishop of Magdeburg, whose ambitions helped trigger the Reformation. His quest for land and power led him to sell papal indulgences, a practice that Martin Luther openly denounced. Paradoxically, Albrecht sympathized with many of Luther's proposed Church reforms. Dürer, who admired both men, engraved this likeness of the prelate in 1519, after he became a cardinal. The sitter was so pleased that he ordered hundreds of prints.

enjoyed in baptism. So glibly enthusiastic was Tetzel that he proclaimed the indulgences could even absolve a man who committed incest.

Luther, long simmering over what he considered a debasement of the Gospel, and increasingly convinced that forgiveness of sins came only through faith and the grace of God and not through the intervention of man, erupted at Tetzel's salesmanship. His theses, intended to bring about a reform of this degrading trade, were interpreted by churchmen as an attack not only on Albrecht's purse but on the papacy and the discipline of the Church. Pope Leo summoned Luther to appear in Rome to answer charges of contumacy and heresy. However, the Elector Frederick managed to have his fellow townsman's case referred to the Imperial Diet, a legislative assembly of the German states scheduled to be held in 1518 in Augsburg. The papal legate, Cardinal Cajetan, a man of great learning and integrity, was sent to give Luther a hearing.

Nuremberg's delegates to the Diet, Caspar Nützel and Lazarus Spengler, were friends of Dürer, and he seems to have had business in Augsburg himself, probably in connection with his work for Maximilian. So he traveled with them to Augsburg; he arrived in June and stayed till September, enjoying the social life, mingling with the great. He made charcoal drawings of many of the notables: Archbishop Albrecht—who was made a cardinal during the Diet—Count Philipp zu Solms, Jacob Fugger the Rich, the artist Hans Burgkmair. Maximilian consulted Dürer on the progress of the *Triumphal Procession,* and on one June afternoon sat for his picture "high up in the palace in his tiny cabinet." Later Dürer made two engravings from his drawing of Albrecht, and from his sketch of Maximilian a woodcut *(page 118)* and two oil paintings. One of the latter, produced after Maximilian's death, manages to combine the Emperor's air of aloof benevolence with the world-weariness of a man nearing the end of the road. He wears a red velvet cape with a wide marten collar and a floppy pointed black hat or beret to which is pinned a holy emblem. His eyes, slanted and set deep behind the high-bridged nose, look at the world obliquely with a restrained melancholy. In his long fingers he holds a pomegranate, which was for him a favorite symbol of immortality.

Dürer did not meet Luther in the brief time the reformer spent at Augsburg under the protection of the Elector Frederick's safe-conduct guarantee. For three days Luther appeared willingly before Cajetan, until it became clear to him that, for all the Cardinal's urbanity, he would be satisfied with nothing less than surrender. Cajetan's instructions were that if Luther did not recant he was to be seized as a heretic and sent to Rome. While Dürer and his companions enjoyed the gay life of the most worldly of German cities, Luther fled Augsburg secretly in his cowl, "without breeches, spurs, stirrups or sword."

Dürer, in fact, never did meet Luther, but he was interested in and later profoundly moved by Luther's protest against the abuses of Rome and by his stern call for a moral re-awakening. Dürer himself, as he approached his 50th year, was possessed by recurrent dark moods, and by fears that he was losing his sight and the skill of his hand—"Dürer is in a bad way," wrote Pirckheimer at this time—and the artist found in Luther's teachings and writings great comfort for his spiritual stress. In his private papers he wrote that Luther was a man "inspired of God" who had "a spirit of the Gospel." In setting forth God's word, Dürer added, Luther "has written more clearly than any that has lived for 140 years."

Dürer sent Luther several of his woodcuts and engravings. He also wrote the Elector Frederick's private secretary asking that the Elector take Luther under his protection "for the sake of Christianity." "For that," he added, "is of more importance to us than all the power and riches of this world. . . . God helping me, if ever I meet Dr. Martin Luther, I intend to draw a careful portrait of him from the life and to engrave it on copper, for a lasting remembrance of a Christian man who helped me out of great distress."

Dürer's sympathy with Luther's reform agitation did not, however, lead him to abjure the traditional Catholic themes in art. In fact, on the very eve of the Reformation Nuremberg seems to have experienced an autumnal flowering of the cult of the Virgin that had so preoccupied the Gothic era, and Dürer painted a number of pictures of the Mother of God. Perhaps the best known is one he painted on commission, a *St. Anne with the Virgin and Child,* sometimes called "Anna Selbdritt," or St. Anne with Two Others *(page 86).* In this picture, Mary, wearing the dress with stiff collar customary for Nuremberg girls of good family, looks no more than an adolescent. Her eyes are almost closed, the pupils just visible, as she looks down with overwhelming love on the small sleeping figure of the Child. Behind and half-leaning on her, one hand on her shoulder, stands St. Anne in the cloak and wimple traditional to Nuremberg women. Beneath the enveloping white cloth only her mouth, her nose and rather bulging eyes are visible. More noteworthy than St. Anne's plain features is the fact that the model for the figure was Dürer's wife Agnes. It was one of the few times that he drew her and the only time he ever painted her in oil.

Late in 1518 the Emperor awarded Dürer a 200-florin bonus, to be paid from the city treasury. But two months later, in January 1519, Maximilian died, and the Nuremberg Council not only refused to pay the bonus, but also declined to continue Dürer's annual pension on the grounds that the contract was no longer binding.

Dürer had counted on the security of his life pension, and now a morbid fear of poverty added to his already troubled state. He took a short holiday in Switzerland to take his mind off his troubles, and on his return made several efforts to draw up a request to the Emperor-elect Charles V to continue his annual stipend or even double it. But since it was expected that Charles at his coronation at Aachen would as a gesture of imperial magnanimity renew old honors, privileges and distinctions, Dürer determined that the best course would be to go to Aachen and to appeal in person to the Emperor and his chancellor, Cardinal Albrecht. He also was glad to avoid a new outbreak of the plague in Nuremberg. So, this time accompanied by his wife, her maid Susanna and baggage that included a great bale of his woodcuts and engravings he intended to sell, Dürer left Nuremberg on July 12, 1520, and set out along the Erlangen road for the Netherlands.

A portrait of Martin Luther, painted in 1526 by Lucas Cranach the Elder, shows the prime mover of the Reformation at the age of 43. Cranach is known as the portraitist of the Reformation because he memorialized not only Luther but many other religious leaders during the half century that he was court painter in Wittenberg, a center of Protestant activity. In this and his other portraits, Cranach's straightforward treatment of his subjects emphasizes their intense and simple piety.

A Monument
in Paper

Of all the works of art conceived to celebrate one man's fame, perhaps none is at once so grandiose and so insubstantial as the Triumphal Arch that Dürer helped to create for the Holy Roman Emperor Maximilian I. A monumental project that required the services of an architect, an iconographer, a master designer and a large company of craftsmen for almost three years, the finished product (*right*) consisted of 192 woodcut prints fitted together to make a single huge print unique in all art: an elaborate arch 11 feet high and 10 feet wide—made entirely of paper.

This curious monument was a fitting memorial to Maximilian, a brilliant but erratic individual who had an unquenchable ambition to be glorified like a Caesar. His budget did not match his aspirations, and so instead of ordering a real Triumphal Arch like those built for victorious Emperors of Rome, Maximilian commissioned Dürer to design a paper one. The result was not only a visual spectacle, but also a celebration of Maximilian's life and virtues. His family tree, for instance, appears above the central portal, while the 24 panels over the other two portals show events of his career. Each niche and panel is freighted with esoteric symbolism that appealed to the intellectual elite of the time. Maximilian• shrewdly capitalized on the medium of printing to circulate his arch far and wide, and despite its flimsy construction it has become an enduring monument to his fame.

The Triumphal Arch of Maximilian I, 1515

So ich d͛
Find ich
New kaise
Des lob ic
Den fürs
Mit sir
Ist sölch
Das er d
All hat z
Als vil i
Der alle
Mit n

loys kung   Ferdinand   Isabella kun   Vladislau ku   Hainrich ku   Joha
zu frankrich king zu ku   gin zu Castili   nig zu hunge   my zu engel   my
gestpt inn vier spani gestwe   geschwegert   rn vii beham   lan de gestwe   gal
den grad   gert im ande   im andern   gestpt im vie   gert im vier   an
              rn grad   grad   den g͛ ad   den gni

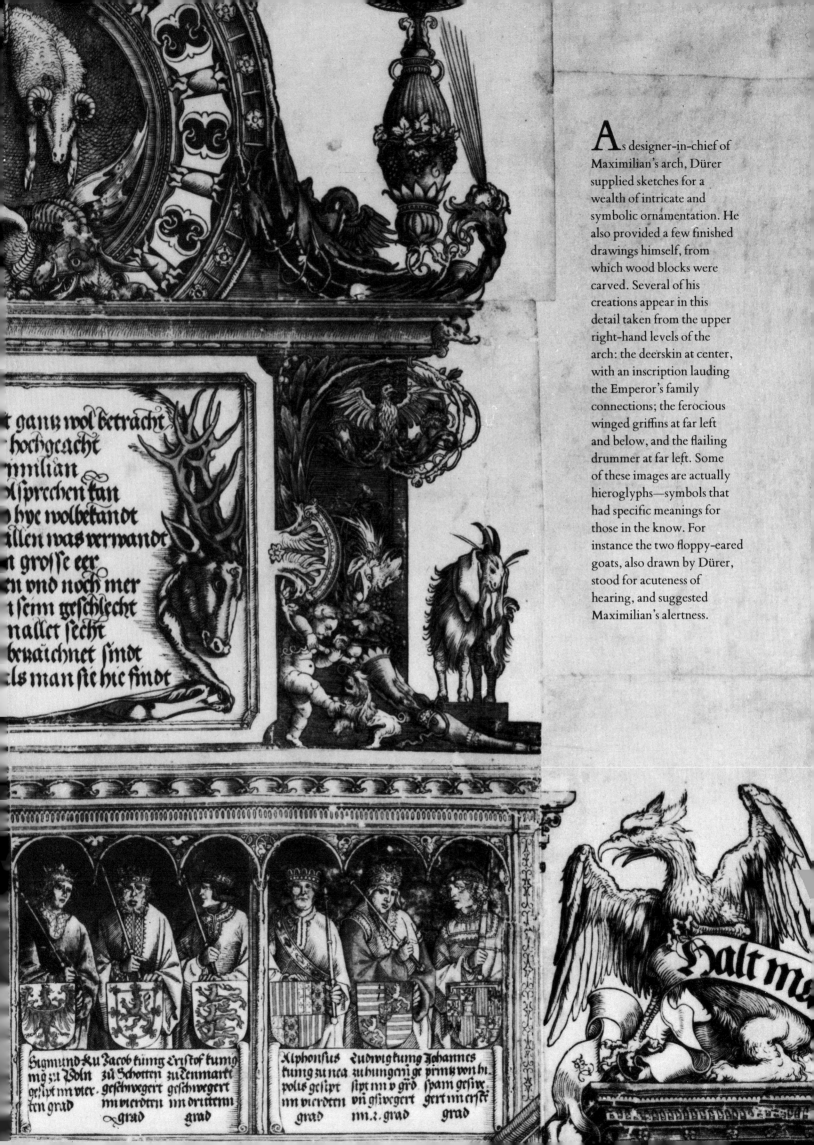

As designer-in-chief of Maximilian's arch, Dürer supplied sketches for a wealth of intricate and symbolic ornamentation. He also provided a few finished drawings himself, from which wood blocks were carved. Several of his creations appear in this detail taken from the upper right-hand levels of the arch: the deerskin at center, with an inscription lauding the Emperor's family connections; the ferocious winged griffins at far left and below, and the flailing drummer at far left. Some of these images are actually hieroglyphs—symbols that had specific meanings for those in the know. For instance the two floppy-eared goats, also drawn by Dürer, stood for acuteness of hearing, and suggested Maximilian's alertness.

t gantz wol betracht
hochgeacht
milian
sprechen kan
hye wolbekandt
illen was verwandt
grosse eer
en vnd noch mer
senn geschlecht
nallet secht
bezaichnet sind
els man sie hie findt

Sigmund ku   Jacob kung   Cristof kung
nig zu Poln   zu Schotten   zu denmarck
gesipt im vier   geschwegert   geschwegert
ten grad   im vierdten   im dritten
grad   grad

Alphonsus   Ludwig kung   Johannes
kung zu nea   zu hungern ge   prins von hi
polis gesipt   sipt im v grd   spani gesiw
im vierdten   vn gswegert   gert im erste
grad   im 2. grad   grad

Halt mo

A Triumphal Arch needs a Triumphal Procession to go with it, so
Maximilian ordered one—also on paper. Another grandiose conception, it
was to have comprised 208 woodcuts joined to make a long, wondrous parade
honoring the Emperor's fame and glory. When Maximilian died in 1519 only
139 of the wood blocks had been carved—but even so the abbreviated
Procession, when it was finally published in 1526, stretched 180 feet.

Dürer was only one of many artists put to work on *The Triumphal
Procession;* his contributions, in fact, consisted of just two woodcuts which,
when put together, depicted the wedding chariot of Maximilian and Mary of
Burgundy. The chariot, driven by a figure representing Victory, carries the
Emperor and his bride. Three women, one holding a huge wedding ring,
stand in front of them, while a sturdy manservant helps push the car.

Like all Dürer's work for Maximilian, these woodcuts, called *The
Burgundian Marriage,* show an unusual facet of his art. Their ornateness, rich
in symbolism and touched by a rare whimsy, presents a vivid contrast to the
sober mood of much of the artist's more familiar work. As purely decorative
art, *The Burgundian Marriage* has a brilliance all its own.

Paul Topler and Martin Pfinzing, 1520

Study of a Dog, 1520

VII

Acclaim in
the Netherlands

Two traveling Nurembergers and a keen-eyed watchdog were among the many subjects Dürer recorded in his small sketchbook during his visit to the Low Countries. He drew in silverpoint, a medium now largely superseded by the modern pencil.

Dürer's visit to the Netherlands with his wife lasted a year. Traveling at a leisurely pace, he carefully jotted down his impressions—where he went, what he did, how much he spent—in a pocket log that served as both diary and account book. Meals, drinks, fares, the occasional evening at gambling, barbers' and bath fees, pictures bought and sold, he kept track of to the last stiver. The souvenirs he bought, the presents he received, the marvels he saw, he never failed to set down, interspersing such ephemera with his personal reflections. With his log he carried a small sketchbook of pink-tinted paper in which he could record in silverpoint what he wished to remember.

The Dürers' first stop after leaving Nuremberg in July 1520 was at Bamberg, where the artist presented the bishop of the city with sets of *The Life of the Virgin* and *The Apocalypse*, some engravings and an oil painting of the Madonna. The bishop in turn paid his bill at the inn, and gave him three letters of introduction and a travel pass that would free him from innumerable toll barriers en route. In the mild summer weather the Dürers moved on by boat to Frankfort and Mainz, and from there down the Rhine gorge through the craggy castled landscape to Cologne. Wherever Dürer went he was recognized, entertained, given ceremonial gifts of wine.

He left the Rhine at Cologne, visited briefly with his cousin, the goldsmith Niklas Dürer, then traveled overland into Netherlandish territory, reaching Antwerp early in August. He put up at the inn of Jobst Planckfelt, which was to be the stopping place for his wife and their maid while he moved about the Low Countries on his affairs. At the inn he made the curious arrangement that he should eat alone or with his host, while the women ate in the "upper kitchen."

Antwerp, the wealthiest and most cosmopolitan city in the Low Countries, was in the midst of festival preparations for the reception of the new Emperor, Maximilian's grandson Charles V, after his coronation. Dürer's arrival, however, was not disregarded. The Painters' Guild promptly tendered him an elaborate banquet at its guild hall: the painters and their wives stood up respectfully when he entered with

Agnes, "as though a great lord were ushered in," he noted in his diary, and afterward escorted him back to his inn in state, with torchlights. Other men of prominence, like the resident Portuguese consul Francisco Bradão, gave dinners in his honor. He was taken to meet the burgomaster and to see the studio of the celebrated painter Quentin Massys.

This pattern of hospitality recurred everywhere he went. All the elite of the Low Countries—men of international affairs, humanist scholars, burgomasters, heads of guilds, physicians, artists—wanted to meet him, entertain him, show off the art treasures of their cities. In Brussels, Bernard van Orley, court painter to Margaret, Regent of the Netherlands, was his host at a meal "so costly," Dürer recorded, "that I do not think 10 florins will pay for it." He viewed the paintings of the "great masters" Rogier van der Weyden in the Town Hall and Hugo van der Goes in the Nassau Chapel. He also inspected the Aztec artifacts that the conqueror Cortez, a subject of Charles V's Spanish realm, had just sent back from Mexico—"the new land of gold," Dürer called it. Two rooms full of armor, weapons, clothing, beds and other objects, including "a sun all of gold a whole fathom broad, and a moon all of silver of the same size," offered tangible evidences of the exciting New World across the Atlantic. "All the days of my life," Dürer wrote, "I have seen nothing that rejoiced my heart so much as these things, for I saw amongst them wonderful works of art, and I marveled at the subtle *Ingenia* of men in foreign lands. Indeed I cannot express all that I thought there."

At Ghent a delegation of painters proudly took him to the Church of St. Bavon to see Jan van Eyck's resplendent altarpiece of the *Adoration of the Lamb,* now almost a century old, and at Bruges, in the Church of Our Lady, he viewed a more recent masterpiece, the marble *Madonna and Child* by Michelangelo, carved in 1503 for a wealthy Bruges merchant who had commissioned it while in Italy. Except to note that Michelangelo was "of Rome," Dürer made no further comment in his diary about his famous Italian contemporary; Michelangelo, by contrast, would one day emphasize his esteem for Dürer by reportedly telling Charles V face to face that if he were not Michelangelo he would rather be Dürer than Emperor.

For all the honors and the ceremonial visits Dürer still found time to gape and collect curios like any tourist. He bought a tortoise-shell shield, an elk's foot, an ox-horn, ivory saltcellars, and engraved goblets. One Lazarus Ravensburger, to whom as a friendly gesture he had given a St. Jerome engraving and a set of his "three large books," gave him in turn "a big fin, five snail shells, four silver and five copper medals, two dried fishes, a white coral, four reed arrows and another white coral."

Dürer went into less detail, regrettably, about some of the curious sights he saw. One was a bed in Brussels that, he noted without amplification, could hold 50 persons; another item, in Antwerp, was an 18-foot skeleton of the "Giant Brabo," a prehistoric monster that had once purportedly ruled the city. Learning of a whale "much more than a hundred fathoms long" that had been stranded by a gale at Zierikzee in Zeeland, Dürer set out in bitterly cold weather to see this wonder. He had to go by boat for the last stage of the trip, and, after being almost shipwrecked, arrived in Zeeland only to discover that the carcass had been washed away by a high tide. On this trip he come down with a violent body-shaking cold that developed into a sickness that would never wholly leave him. He described one recurring attack as "a violent fever, with great weakness, nausea, and headache."

Dürer's fascination with animals can be seen in a number of his Netherlands sketches—of a grumpy walrus captured off the Flemish coast, of dogs small and large (page 136), of a live lion in a zoo at Ghent. For the privilege of drawing this beast (back end papers), so different from the imagined lions of his earlier works, he tipped its keepers three stivers, duly noting the sum in his diary.

Everywhere his deft hand recorded what he saw: not only animals but also people, curiosities, buildings and occasionally landscapes, including a remarkably free pen-and-ink study of the River Scheldt at Antwerp, with docked sailing vessels. He produced over a hundred portraits of both the famous and the humble: a sketch and a charcoal drawing of that arch-priest of the old learning and the new scholarship, Erasmus of Rotterdam; silverpoint sketches of two visiting Nuremberg dignitaries, Martin Pfinzing and Paul Topler (page 136), of the brutal-faced Imperial Herald Caspar Sturm, of an open-faced young man who may have been the painter Lucas van Leyden, and of Catherine, the Negro maid of the Portuguese consul; and a brush drawing of a nameless 93-year-old citizen of Antwerp. Dürer used the infinitely wrinkled features of this subject as a model for an oil painting of St. Jerome at his reading desk, one finger resting meditatively on a skull (page 87). This work, painted for the Portuguese ambassador, is the most striking of the oils Dürer executed in the Netherlands, the one that stirred the most attention at the time.

Between sketching and painting and conducting a brisk trade in prints Dürer did not lose sight of the main economic objective of his journey from Nuremberg: the renewal of the pension granted him by the late Emperor Maximilian. Margaret, the Regent of the Netherlands, was Maximilian's daughter, and it was to her that Dürer initially addressed his campaign. He sent her a complete set of his prints and engravings, also shrewdly seeing to it that her treasurer received his own set of The Engraved Passion. Margaret invited Dürer to her court at Mechlin and, as he recorded in his diary, was "quite exceptionally kind to me," agreeing to mention his pension problem to the new Emperor, Charles V, her nephew.

Dürer next pursued the matter by traveling to Aachen, the traditional coronation city of the Holy Roman Emperors, for the crowning of Charles V in October 1520. He attended the ceremony, noting that it was "more magnificent than anything that those who live in our parts have ever seen," and he also sketched the cathedral with its porphyry columns, taken from imperial Roman buildings, that the Emperor Charlemagne had had brought from Ravenna when he built his palace at Aachen in the early Ninth Century. But the occasion scarcely provided Dürer with an opportunity to press his private petitions. Not until he had gone on with the Emperor's retinue to Cologne did he finally—after "great toil and trouble"—have his wish fulfilled. From Cardinal Albrecht he received a document signed by Charles V renewing his pension for life and granting him the amount unpaid by the Nuremberg Council since Maximilian's death.

A few months later Charles V was to attend to a far more momentous matter, presiding over the Imperial Diet at Worms to which Martin Luther had been summoned to defend himself against the heresy charges prepared against him in Rome. Luther had already burned one papal bull threatening him with excommunication. Now, standing before the Catholic Habsburg Emperor in the tense and crowded hall, he appealed finally from popes and councils to Scripture and plain reason, concluding with the ringing words: "Here I stand; God help me. I cannot do otherwise." After a number of Diet members had left, including some who favored Luther, the rest promulgated the Edict of Worms, condemning him and setting in motion a second papal bull, as yet unpublished, that formally excommunicated him. Fearing for Luther's safety, the Elector Frederick had him intercepted on his return journey to Wittenberg, spirited him away in a feigned abduction, and secreted him in the derelict castle of Wartburg.

A rumor raced through the Low Countries that the vanished Luther had been murdered. Dürer was in Antwerp when he heard it. "Oh God," he wrote in his notebook with somber passion, "if Luther is dead, who will now explain the Gospel to us? What might he not have written for us in the next ten or twenty years? Oh all ye pious Christian men, help me deeply to bewail this man, inspired of God, and to pray Him again to send us an enlightened man . . . Oh ye Christian men, pray God for help, for His judgment draweth nigh and His justice shall appear. Then shall we behold the innocent blood which the Pope, Priests, Bishops and Monks have shed, judged and condemned. These are the slain who lie beneath the Altar of God and cry for vengeance, to whom the voice of God answereth: 'Await the full number of the innocent slain, then will I judge.'"

Yet though Dürer could privately denounce "the un-Christian papacy, which strives with its heavy load of human laws against the redemption of Christ," he could not, like his more belligerent friend Pirckheimer, break with the tradition of the Church in which his parents had died. He continued to go to Mass and confession (he noted that at one Mass in Antwerp his wife had her purse stolen); he remained on amicable terms with Cardinal Albrecht and other high churchmen; he delighted in the familiar ceremonies of the Church, and the worship of the Blessed Virgin in Antwerp's colorful religious procession "the Sunday after Our Dear Lady's Assumption." He would never actually meet Luther, and he would never formally sever his connection with the Catholic Church.

As the summer of 1521 approached, the Antwerp Council—like the Venetian Senate 15 years earlier—tried to persuade Dürer to settle there, offering him a house, a yearly stipend of 300 Philips gulden, and freedom from taxation. But he could no more consider abandoning his "honorable town" for the Low Countries than for Italy. He began to make his preparations for returning home. He paid a visit to the Regent Margaret at Mechlin. Having already given her sets of his prints and engravings and made her two delicate drawings on vellum, this time he brought as a gift his portrait of Maximilian. But when he offered it to her she refused to accept it, apparently finding it a poor likeness. With chill politeness, she let him see her library and her collection of paintings. Aware that his old Venice acquaintance Jacopo de' Barbari had ended his life as her court painter, he asked if he might have "Master Jacob's little book," which he hoped might contain the still-elusive secret of bodily measurements and proportions. She refused, saying that she had already promised it to her present painter, Bernard van Orley. The disappointed Dürer recorded that "she never gave anything for what I had presented to and made for her."

Returning to Antwerp, he packed his acquisitions and his various gifts to friends at home: "a large cap, an ink-stand of buffalo horn, a silver emperor, a pound of pistachios and three sugar canes" for Pirckheimer; an elk's foot for Caspar Nützel; for the Spenglers "a good pair of gloves . . . a bag and three fine horns each"; and for his patrician friends on the Nuremberg Council, Jacob Muffel and Hieronymus Holzschuher, respectively, a scarlet breast-cloth and a large horn. "In all my doings, spendings, sales and other dealings, in all my connections with high and low, I have suffered loss in the Netherlands," he observed in his diary. He settled with his innkeeper, gave the man's wife a florin—he had already painted her—and tipped the servants.

He was on the point of leaving when King Christian II of Denmark, brother-in-law of Charles V, sent for him. The "Nero of the North"—so called for his massacres of the Swedes—had just arrived in Antwerp on his way to Brussels. Learning of Dürer's presence, he asked to be sketched. Dürer drew "the manly, handsome man" in charcoal, and the King was so pleased with the finished work that he invited the artist to dinner and insisted on taking him to Brussels so that Dürer could paint him in oils. He completed the portrait—since lost—in a week, and was well rewarded; Christian gave him 30 gold florins. There was a side benefit as well: Dürer was invited to attend the banquet the King gave for the Emperor Charles, his aunt Margaret and his sister, Queen Eleonore of Portugal.

Just a year to the day after starting out from Nuremberg, the Dürers left Brussels for home. They traveled overland to Aachen and Cologne, and from there by boat up the Rhine. At Cologne Dürer again stayed with his cousin Niklas. It may have been at this time that he drew his wife and a little girl in Cologne costume in his sketchbook. This silverpoint, showing a solid, shrewish Agnes, her lips pursed as she stares away from the girl with a look of sour discontent, explains the Dürers' relationship better than words can. Some time during the Netherlands stay Dürer had made a larger drawing of his wife, on purple-grounded paper, in which she appears plumper, less forbidding, but still purse-mouthed, and scarcely more attractive.

When Dürer saw the towers of Nuremberg again he was, at 50, prematurely aged, failing in health and uncertain in energy. Before he left

"Expulsion from Paradise"

"The Rich Man"

"The Ploughman"

the Netherlands he had planned to produce a new Passion series of woodcuts, for he noted in his diary: "I have made three *Bearings of the Cross* and two *Agonies in the Garden* on five half-sheets." Four of these drawings survive, but the only woodcut that he completed of the projected series was the print of the *Last Supper*. Back in his workshop in the Zistelgasse he made a number of drawings and studies for an altarpiece of the Madonna and Child surrounded by saints, ancestors, relatives and musical angels—a set-piece called by the Italians, who originated the theme, a "sacred conversation"—and a large engraving of a Crucifixion with mutiple figures. But these pictures, like the woodcut series, were never completed.

The Nuremberg Council welcomed Dürer's return by commissioning him to paint three large pictures needed to redecorate the long wall of the Town Hall's Assembly Room. He accepted the task but his spirit was not in it. For a central picture he sketched a crowd of pipers in a balcony and padded it on either side with the familiar humanist theme of the calumny of the ancient Greek painter Apelles and with his old drawing of Maximilian's Triumphal Car. Only the designs, however, were Dürer's. The actual painting was done by his apprentice Georg Pencz, and by other pupils.

What Dürer had become, how he had come to feel about himself, can be seen in his last self-portrait, a metalpoint drawing of a nude Man of Sorrows that he made in 1522. He sits slumped forward, arms crossed, one hand holding the whip and the other the scourge of the Passion. The once robust and still muscular frame is wasted, the elbows sharp-edged, the stomach muscles sagging. Strings of hair wisp about his balding head and scraggly beard, and his turned-down mouth shows his broken teeth. Above the withered neck and hunched shoulders, the eyes no longer look forward but apprehensively to the side. Here the gloved gallant of 1498, the later decorous imitator of Christ, has become a man naked before God, stripped of the concealments of fur and velvet, accepting and enduring the underlying sorrow that is woven into the very fabric of man's being.

The half-dozen years remaining to Dürer, while marked by his physical decline, were nevertheless a time of fruition, a brilliant period of portraiture that had already begun with the concentration of character seen in the sketches in the Netherlands, and that was to end with the masterpiece of *The Four Apostles*. No longer in his later portraits did Dürer feel the need of a landscape background, or even the half-length display of his sitters as in the portrait of Maximilian. Just as he had done with himself as a Man of Sorrows, so now with his models he disregarded all the trappings to let the essential features stand out in stark clarity.

This high period culminated in his two most celebrated portraits, those of the Nuremberg patricians, the Councilor Hieronymus Holzschuher and the Burgomaster Jacob Muffel. These worthies stare from the canvas, their civic pride undimmed in the four centuries since they were painted, the stout burgher breed that had resisted knights and margraves and even emperors. The very syllables of their names—in English, Woodenshoer and Muzzle—ring with bourgeois bluntness. Their light-blue background forms a deliberately nonaristocratic contrast to the cool green against which the aloof Maximilian toys with the pomegranate, the symbol of his own immortality and that of his house.

Holzschuher's bearded full face—the high forehead with the thinning white curls, the gleaming eyes and lively mouth—is that of a man of action, quick to anger. One can imagine him leading a militia band to hunt down a robber knight like Götz of the Iron Fist; one cannot imagine him as a courtier or in a monk's cowl. Burgomaster Muffel's shaven face is more austere and withdrawn and beneath the long nose the thin lips are capable of restraining anger. Poised in his velvet skullcap and marten collar, he is more the grave weigher of decisions than the doer, the necessary counterpart to the choleric and energetic Holzschuher. Together they are Nuremberg incarnate.

Dürer's last great individual oil portrait is of Johann Kleberger, a wealthy young man of mysterious background who married Pirckheimer's favorite daughter, Felicitas, over her father's furious objections and a few days after the wedding abandoned her to go to France, where he lived until his death, eventually giving away all his wealth to the poor. The picture is painted within a circle in a singular antique manner as if it were a bust. Kleberger's shoulders and neck are bare, his face as sharply defined as if it were cut by a sculptor's chisel. He stares into space with fixed eyes, a visionary—as Dürer has captured him—with whom no human contact, even that of his wife, would be possible.

While Dürer in Nuremberg was painting the last of his portraits, the primacy of German art was beginning to pass to other, more vigorous hands. Lucas Cranach the Elder, although only a year younger than Dürer, was destined to outlive him by almost three decades, and in the 1520s was still at the peak of his powers. Dürer's old patron, the Elector Frederick, had brought Cranach from his native Franconia in 1505 to be court painter at Wittenberg. There he would serve Frederick and his successors for nearly half a century, not only producing numerous portraits of them—in one year he painted Frederick 60 times—but also designing coins and medals and festival costumes for them, decorating their palaces, even choosing color schemes for suites of rooms. In return for such assiduous services Frederick ennobled Cranach, so that he was able henceforth to sign his pictures with a crest of his own devising—a winged serpent. Overwhelmed with commissions, he became the richest citizen and landowner of Wittenberg, and yet, at the age of 80, loyally followed the incumbent elector into exile in the wake of a power struggle with the Emperor Charles V.

Cranach was the perfect court painter, satisfied to please the eye without ruffling the mind, delighting in minutiae, a virtuoso equally facile at portraiture and landscapes and nudes, at religious and secular themes. He never tired of repeating his naked Eves and Dianas and Lucretias and Venuses, and the older he grew, the younger and more immature he painted them *(page 170)*. But while his fame rests in part on these delicately sensuous females, it also rests, paradoxically, on his role as the portraitist of the Reformation. Luther had been court preacher at Wittenberg even as Cranach was court painter, and after the Elector Fred-

"The Mariner"

"The Merchant"

"The Abbot"

"The Abbess"

erick gave the reformer his political protection, the bond became even closer. It is through the many portraits of Luther and his circle turned out by Cranach and his workshop to meet a growing demand that Cranach has come down to us as the artist-champion of the new Protestantism.

These portraits are, however, essentially stereotypes, more precise than probing. Dürer's only real rival in portraiture was not Cranach but a German of the generation following theirs: Hans Holbein the Younger. It was to fall to Holbein to perfect his great gift for dispassionate observation in a foreign land. Living in England from 1532 until his death in 1543, and Painter Royal for the latter half of that period, Holbein sketched and painted King Henry VIII and his wives and court and brought an entire age to life *(pages 147-155).* His solid, fleshy Henry is the only Henry we can now conceive of. His Anne of Cleves and Jane Seymour, his churchmen and his lords, remain as real as faces to be seen on London's streets today. To a period of English history he has given the fourth dimension of time.

Dürer had been the first German to come under the spell of the new theories of Italian art, with all the psychological tension involved in moving from the world of the late Gothic to that of the Renaissance. For Holbein, born 26 years after Dürer in 1497, there was no such tension; finding the paths laid out, he had merely to follow them. His birthplace was Augsburg, the most Italianate of German cities. His artist father, Hans Holbein the Elder, influenced by the works of van der Weyden and Schongauer, had shifted from Gothic expressionism to the exact rendering of what was before him. He made some of the most remarkable life sketches of his day, but there was as yet little demand for portraiture and he drew these sketches for his solitary satisfaction rather than for financial gain. When his son was still a child he enthusiastically trained him in the Italian Renaissance manner and style, and encouraged him to develop his objective eye.

For the younger Holbein, the road to London lay through Basel. He arrived there in 1515, at the age of 18, like any journeyman seeking his fortune, willing to try his trained hand at anything, even sign painting. Although he undertook a number of religious pictures, including the Passion and the haunting *Body of Christ in the Tomb,* before he had been in Basel a year he had begun to show his mastery of portraiture, as in the likenesses of Burgomaster Jacob Mayer and his wife Dorothea. At 21 he made the astonishingly vital picture of Bonifacius Amerbach of the noted printing family, inscribing proudly on its surface: "Though but a painted face I do not deviate from life and my true lines give a noble portrait of my master."

Several years before Holbein, Erasmus of Rotterdam had come to Basel to arrange with its celebrated printer, Johannes Froben, for the publication of his edition of the New Testament—the first to be printed in Greek. Since Holbein sometimes drew woodcut designs for Froben, it is probable that the young artist and the middle-aged humanist met at the printer's. When Erasmus' satirical *Praise of Folly* was published shortly after the New Testament, Holbein made 82 marginal illustrations in the author's private copy. Over the next years he sketched and painted the austere scholar a number of times. Their friendship deepened, and in 1526 Erasmus helped decide Holbein's future course. In an excess of zeal, the stricter Protestants of Basel began to object to the use of pictures in churches, and even to the luxury of secular paintings in private homes, thus depriving painters of a major source of income. That year Holbein went off to England with a letter of recommendation from Erasmus to his humanist friend, the influential Sir Thomas More, soon to be England's Lord Chancellor; in Basel, the letter explained, "the arts are out in the cold." Holbein remained in England for two years, returned to Basel to find the spirit of iconoclasm even stronger than before, and in 1532, despite the pleas of the city council that he stay, departed for his new homeland for good.

P erhaps the most instructive approach to the differences between Holbein and Dürer as portraitists lies in their separate studies of Erasmus. Holbein, in his three most notable paintings of his friend—made in 1523 in Basel—fixed the enduring conception of Erasmus we now have: the ironic Catholic rationalist and arch-scholar, priestly in demeanor, with sharp nose, wide mouth and hooded eyes, an aristocrat of the book, devoid of any passion but that of learning.

Three years later—after Erasmus had asked through their mutual friend Pirckheimer if Dürer would draw his likeness again—Dürer made an engraving of Erasmus based on the charcoal sketch that he had made in the summer of 1520 in Antwerp. The work shows Erasmus standing and writing at a lectern. In front of it is a vase of violets and lilies of the valley; to its side are four books, one of them open. Dürer has limned the form and face of Erasmus with his usual mastery, but the effect is more interpretive than representational. The artist has concentrated less on a meticulous rendering of his subject's every feature than on an idealization of a great scholar, surrounded by symbols of learning and of natural beauty. Choosing only those aspects of Erasmus that he wished to emphasize, Dürer has produced a selective characterization to which the viewer must add his own imaginings of the scholar's personality. The Greek inscription behind Erasmus stresses this point; for a better image of him, it says in part, one must go to his writings. Erasmus himself was disappointed with the portrait, writing Pirckheimer: "Dürer has portrayed me, but it is not at all like me." However, he added, "I am no longer the man I was five years ago!"

Inevitably one is drawn to a comparison between Dürer and Holbein, and yet the comparison founders in the difference of their approach. Holbein drew what he saw with scientific detachment, a marvelous but cold regard. Both his intention and his accomplishment are inscribed in the portrait frontispiece to the works of Erasmus: "If anyone has not seen Erasmus, this portrait, drawn skillfully from life, gives his image." Dürer had other intentions. He put too much of his own feelings and beliefs into his work to confine it wholly within factual images. What he did in his portraits was to fulfill the qualities that remained latent or unfulfilled in the lives of his sitters. Dürer saw them not only as they were but as they might be. His portraits are neither cool likenesses nor flattery, but inner realization.

Desiderius Erasmus, the great humanist scholar, was portrayed in late middle age by both Dürer and Hans Holbein the Younger. Dürer's idealized engraving of Erasmus (*above*), showing him amid his books and papers, proved less to the scholar's liking than Holbein's more realistic painting (*below*).

"The Mirror Is Our Teacher"

Dürer's countryman and contemporary, Hans Holbein, the finest portraitist of the 16th Century and one of the finest of all time, found success not in his native Germany but in Switzerland and England. Born in 1497, Holbein was trained as a painter by his father, a leading artist in Augsburg. But while still in his teens he went to live in Basel, an important center for art and humanist scholarship. Except for brief trips to Italy and France, Holbein remained there for about 11 years, and achieved a wide range of success. He illustrated books and produced woodcut designs; he painted murals, frescoes, altarpieces and decorated the façades of buildings; he even made designs for jewelry, tableware and stained-glass windows.

In the mid-1520s, however, life for an artist in Basel became difficult. Zealous Protestant reformers removed paintings from churches and monasteries and destroyed them, and no new religious art was commissioned. Faced with unemployment, Holbein decided to travel to England, where he went recommended by a friend, the scholar Erasmus. There, he became a court painter to Henry VIII and produced splendid royal portraits. As a portraitist, Holbein followed Leonardo da Vinci's dictum, "The mirror is our teacher." And, indeed, Holbein faced himself (*right*) as well as other subjects with uncompromising objectivity, recording with truth and clarity the likenesses of 16th Century man.

Relatively little is known of Holbein's private life and personality, but the steadfast, penetrating eyes of this stern self-portrait suggest a perceptive observer of humanity. At the time he painted this picture, Holbein was 45; less than a year later he died of the plague in London.

Hans Holbein the Younger: *Self-Portrait, 1542-1543*

IOANNES HOLPENIVS BA— SILEENSIS

SVI IPSIVS EFFIGIATOR Æ: XLV.

Holbein the Younger: *Dorothea Kannengiessen*, c. 1526

Holbein the Younger: *Jacob Meyer*, c. 1526

One of Holbein's finest religious paintings was created in Basel, in 1526, when Jacob Meyer, a wealthy Catholic banker and former burgomaster of the city, defied the proscription against such pictures and asked the artist to paint an altarpiece for the chapel of his country estate. In the customary fashion, the artist portrayed the donor and his family *(right)* kneeling reverently before the Madonna, who spreads her robe protectively while the Infant blesses the devout group.

Before starting the painting Holbein made extensive color notes and detailed drawings both of the banker and his second wife *(left)*. These were made in colored chalk, with which Holbein was able to render many of the delicate tones and subtle shadings of expression that appear in his finished painting. Indeed, in the drawing of Meyer, Holbein has already captured the intensity and piety of the man's face.

Two years after his completion of the picture, on his return to Basel from a trip to England, Holbein altered the painting at Meyer's request. The banker's daughter *(right, foreground)* had originally been portrayed as a young girl. Holbein repainted her, slightly older, in her wedding dress. He also added to the composition a portrait of Meyer's first wife (seen in profile behind the second wife) so that the entire family would be shown.

Holbein the Younger: *Madonna of Mercy and the Family of Jacob Meyer,* c. 1526

Holbein the Younger: *Sir Thomas More,* 1527

Shortly after painting the Meyer altarpiece, Holbein traveled to England, where the philosopher-statesman Thomas More helped to launch his career. Holbein painted a group portrait of More's family, which has been lost, and a brooding study of More himself *(above),* realistically depicted with a light stubble of beard. More's face reflects the dignity and determination of a man who would one day be executed for his refusal to condone Henry VIII's

Holbein the Younger: *The Artist's Family,* 1528-1529

capricious establishment of a new church in England.

Before settling in England permanently, Holbein returned to Basel, where he had left his family. While there, he painted the dolorous picture above, in which the neglect and financial hardships his wife and children had suffered during his absence are pitifully evident. The artist abruptly left them once again to return to England. When he died, he left no mention of them in his will.

Holbein the Younger: *King Henry VIII*, 1536

Jane Seymour, 1536

Anne of Cleves, 1539

Catherine Howard, 1540-1541

While serving Henry VIII, Holbein painted portraits of three of the King's six wives, an ill-fated series of ladies whose fates are recounted in the couplet: "Divorced, beheaded, died/ Divorced, beheaded, survived."

Henry's third wife, Jane Seymour *(above, left)* died after giving birth to the King's heir Edward, whom Holbein painted as a child of two *(right).* While helping to scout new brides, Holbein painted Anne of Cleves *(top, center),* whom Henry married and soon divorced. The most beautiful of the King's wives painted by Holbein was Catherine Howard *(top, right),* who reigned for only 15 months. Like her infamous cousin, Anne Boleyn, Henry's second wife, Catherine was beheaded for adultery.

Holbein painted the King himself several times. The portrait shown at left is the first, thought to have been completed as a test before the artist was named court painter. After proving himself, Holbein supplied the high-living monarch with portraits, designs for silverware, jewelry, weapons and even Henry's own lavish clothing.

Holbein the Younger: *Edward VI as a Child,* 1539

One of Holbein's greatest achievements is his monumental double portrait of the French Ambassador to England, Jean de Dinteville, with his friend Bishop Georges de Selve. In addition to incisive personality studies of the elegant de Dinteville *(left)* and the restrained de Selve, Holbein painted a virtual catalogue of the artistic and philosophical interests of these two intellectuals. In meticulous perspective, Holbein included such diverse paraphernalia as a celestial globe, a lute with a broken string, a Lutheran hymnbook, a pair of compasses, flutes, a crucifix and a sundial—some of which are shown in the detail at right below.

The most remarkable object in the painting, however, is a grotesquely distorted pattern that seems to grow out of the lower edge of the frame. Unrecognizable when the painting is viewed from the front at eye level, the object

Holbein the Younger: *The Ambassadors,* 1533

takes shape when it is seen from below, near the right corner of the picture. It seems that the painting was meant to be hung high on a wall, perhaps over a doorway, so that when viewers passed beneath it the distorted object would become recognizable. What they saw was a skull, shown at right in an optically corrected photograph. The skull is thought to represent de Dinteville's morbid philosophical preoccupation with death.

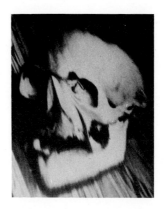

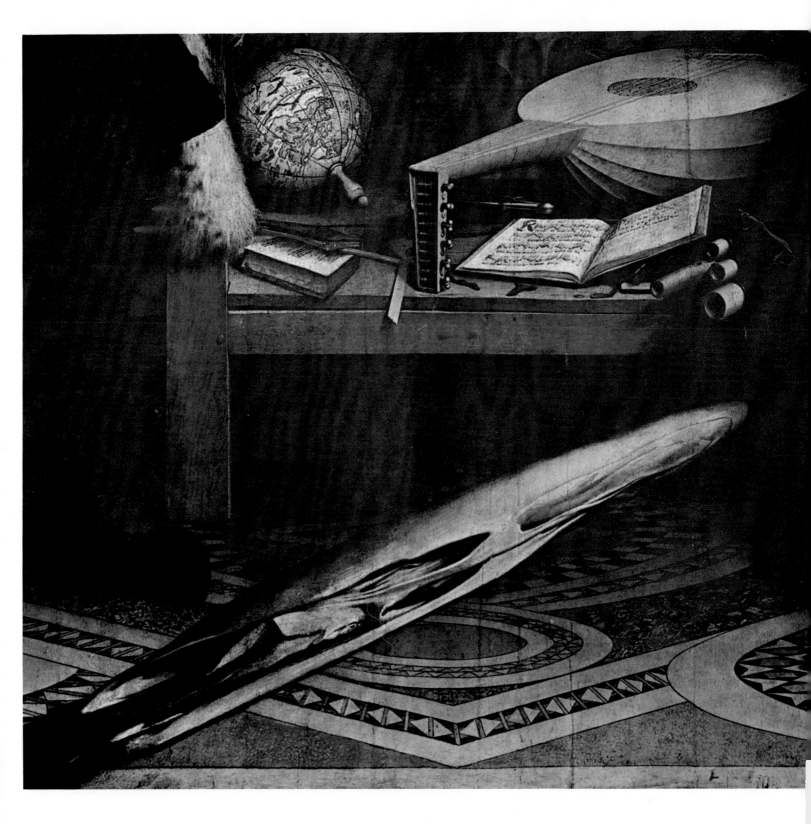

ALBRECHT DÜRER, 1471-1528 JOHANNES UND PETRUS

ALBRECHT DÜRER, 1471-1528 PAULUS UND MARCUS

156

VIII

A Bequest
of Theory

Dürer's great masterpiece, the double panel called *The Four Apostles,* contrasts the features and temperaments of four saints: *(left to right)* John the Evangelist, Peter, Mark and Paul. The text at the bottom of the panels, added at Dürer's direction and testifying to his conservative faith, admonishes the more radical followers of Luther and urges an end to the divisive arguments that were splitting Nuremberg into warring religious camps.

The Four Apostles, 1526

In Nuremberg, as elsewhere in Europe, the consequences of the breach between Martin Luther and the Church of Rome were quickly felt. Pirckheimer and another friend of Dürer's, Lazarus Spengler, were singled out for excommunication for their espousal of Luther's doctrines. Everywhere within the city's walls these doctrines were hotly debated. Propaganda poured from both sides. Hans Sachs, Nuremberg's cobbler-poet, came out in vociferous doggerel for the new Bible-directed faith, and the monastery of Luther's own Augustinian Order became a center for its propagation. Ordinary citizens grew increasingly sympathetic to it, although the magistrates tried as long as possible to avoid committing themselves to either side for fear of civil war.

As Lutheran sentiment rose, the old faith found itself in defensive retreat. Masses for the dead were neglected. Holy water fonts ran dry. The city authorities abolished the traditional Passion and Mystery Plays. No longer was the reliquary containing the skull of Nuremberg's patron saint, St. Sebald, carried through the streets. Only reluctantly did the councilors allow the display at the annual Relics Fair of 1524 of such imperial treasures as pieces of the tablecloth used at the Last Supper. They made this decision under the threat of violence by pilgrims to the city, most of whom were country folk and staunchly orthodox.

With the rising tide of religious conflict, radical leaders sprang up, pushing the new teachings to extremes that were to dismay Luther himself. The rector of St. Sebald's School came forward to deny the truth even of the Scriptures. Under his influence three of Dürer's assistants— including Georg Pencz, who had married Dürer's maid Susanna— went further and denied the person of God and Christ, declared themselves atheists and communists, and were expelled from the city.

The challenge to the established order spilled over from religious to social and economic matters as well. The humble class that the burghers called "Hans behind the wall" was more restive than ever. In 1525 the alarmed patrician council ordered the execution of an innkeeper and a journeyman for inciting their followers to free themselves from the burdens imposed by their betters. Unrest over oppressive taxes and the harsh conditions of daily life was not an urban phenomenon alone. The peasants of southern and central Germany, threatening lords and commoners alike, banded together under the Bundschuh, a political movement named after the coarse boot that was the emblem of their revolt. Armed bands roved the countryside sacking monasteries and abbeys, burning villages and putting townspeople to the sword, devastating the landscape up to the very walls of Nuremberg itself.

The heavens themselves threatened, for in that year all the planets appeared within the constellation of Pisces, the Fish. Nurembergers waited fearfully for another Deluge, perhaps for the Last Judgment. Some in their prudent anxiety tried to anticipate the new flood by reserving lodgings on the tops of houses, and there was even talk of moving the government to the mountains.

Nuremberg Lutherans and Catholics were ordered by the Emperor Charles to debate their differences in the Town Hall. There, in March 1525, in the presence of the papal legate and the Emperor's representative and brother, the Archduke Ferdinand of Austria, the Grand Council after the debate announced its separation from the Church of Rome. Ferdinand had earlier alerted his brother to the possibility of such an outcome. "Luther's doctrine has taken such deep root," he had written, "that among a thousand persons there is not one who is not to some extent touched by it."

In the wake of the Council's decision came a number of municipal edicts suppressing monasteries and pre-empting their buildings and libraries for public use. Dürer, long moved by Luther's teachings but still respectful of the tradition of the old, took no active part in the controversy. As a city-bred artist he had scant understanding or sympathy for the conditions that were bringing the desperate peasants to revolt. But he was much troubled by the agony of the times as well as by the inner conflict of his own religious beliefs. For him, as for ordinary men, the conjunction of the planets was a presage of disaster. Always vision-haunted, he was so distressed by a dream he had of a second Deluge that on waking he made a watercolor sketch of it.

His *Dream Vision,* as he called it, shows a hilly autumnal landscape with a distant village, indicated in a kind of painter's shorthand. Behind the village ominous spirals of water pour from the sky with cyclonic force, while in the center a darkly radiant water-mass reaching from heaven to earth expands like the mushrooming cloud of an atomic explosion, moving to obliterate the village and the landscape and finally the very globe. From this dream Dürer awoke trembling all over and after immediately sketching what he had seen, wrote below it:

"In the year 1525, at Whitsun between Wednesday and Pentecost, during the night in my sleep I saw this vision, how great waters fell from the sky. And the first fell to the earth about four miles from me with much force and with a great roar and spray, drowning the whole earth. At this I was so afraid that I awoke before the other waters fell. And the waters which fell were very great. Some fell far away, some nearer, and they fell from such a great height that they seemed to be falling with the same speed. But when the first water which fell upon the earth had almost reached me, the wind began to blow with such violence that I woke and was so terrified that my whole body trembled and it was long before I came to myself. But when I got up in the morning I painted it above, just as I had seen it. May God turn all things for the best."

It was in the resolution of this mood that he now labored on his *Four Apostles,* the culmination of his work as a painter, committing himself privately to the cause of Luther as he did so. Under each figure he placed passages from the Apostles' writings, selected from the translation of the New Testament that Luther had made in the Wartburg. The Nuremberg calligrapher Johannes Neudörffer inscribed the texts and Dürer's own prefatory words of warning:

"All worldly rulers in these dangerous times should give good heed that they receive not human misguidance for the Word of God, for God will have nothing added to His Word nor taken away from it. Hear therefore these four excellent men, Peter, John, Paul and Mark, their warning. . . ."

The wings of Giovanni Bellini's *Madonna Enthroned with Four Saints,* admired by Dürer as a young artist on his first visit to Venice 30 years earlier, may have given him the basis of the conception of *The Four Apostles.* But the roots of the picture penetrated deeply into the fiber of Dürer's artistic life. One can trace them in engravings that he made of St. Paul and St. Thomas in 1514, of St. Bartholomew and St. Simon in 1523, of St. Philip in 1526. But in the great painting the outward irradiation of the haloes of the saints of the earlier works has been replaced by the inner light of faith.

A quality of strength that defies explanation, that is felt rather than defined, is what has made the picture endure as a work of art. One feels it as one sees the four larger-than-lifesize figures for the first time in their actuality, on a wall of Munich's Alte Pinakothek. Reproductions

Dürer once wrote that he often dreamed of "great art" he might produce but that he could not remember these dreams when he awoke. On the night of June 7, 1525, however, he had a nightmare about the end of the world that he vividly recalled. He recaptured part of it in this watercolor showing the earth menaced by huge, dark clouds of rain. The foreboding which this scene aroused, mentioned in his notes below, was underscored by widespread predictions that year of a great flood that would rival even the Biblical deluge.

have made them familiar, but one is still not prepared for the over-powering sense of vital humanity, what Goethe called "the incredible greatness" of these exalted figures.

With the completion of *The Four Apostles* in 1526 Dürer's time was running out. The inventiveness of his earlier years, so apparently inexhaustible, had failed him as his body was now failing him. During the year and a half that he still had to live he abandoned all work except the theoretical writings which he had begun more than a decade before. In the eyes of a distressed Pirckheimer he seemed a living skeleton, "withered as a bundle of straw."

Conscious of approaching death, Dürer wanted to leave behind for other artists a sure guide such as he himself had never been able to find in his youth. "For," he explained in the dedication of one of his books, "it is evident that though the German painters are not a little skillful with the hand and in the use of colors, they have as yet been wanting in the arts of measurement, perspective, and other like matters. It is therefore to be hoped that if they learn these also and gain skill by knowledge and knowledge by skill, they will in time allow no other nation to take the prize before them."

Just as Luther had had to forge his own language in his German translation of the Bible, so Dürer had to create for his purposes a technical language up to then nonexistent. His humanist friends wrote in Latin; Dürer's use of the vernacular—an eccentric choice, in their opinion— was the first attempt at scientific German. Of his three technical books, two were completed and published in his lifetime. His first, *Introduction in the Art of Measurement with Compass and Ruler,* illustrated with woodcuts and printed in 1525, was dedicated to Pirckheimer. In it he dealt with problems of linear geometry, two-dimensional figures, three-dimensional bodies and theoretical perspective, intending it as a thoroughly serviceable guide, one that could be understood and used not only by painters, but also by "goldsmiths, sculptors, stonemasons, joiners, and all who require measurements" in their daily work. No one, Dürer went on to say, was "obliged to avail himself of this doctrine of mine, but I am sure that whosoever does adopt it . . . will pursue the search and discover far more than I now point out."

Of even more immediate practical concern was his small illustrated *Teaching about the Fortification of Towns, Castles and Places* that he published in 1527, dedicating it to the Archduke Ferdinand, then in charge of Charles V's Habsburg possessions. Both date and dedication were pertinent, for in that year the King of France was again at war with the Emperor, imperial troops had sacked Rome and Ferdinand faced the task of fortifying Vienna. Having had experience as an eyewitness at a siege by Nurembergers of the Castle of Hohenasperg in 1519, Dürer was aware of how artillery and other innovations of the Renaissance had changed the art of war. With these changes in mind he described various advantageous kinds of forts, blockhouses and fortifications, and the mounting of artillery. His section on the construction of a fortified capital is really an introduction to town planning, with regulations laid down for street-networks, houses, stables, factories, breweries, marketplaces, inns, and

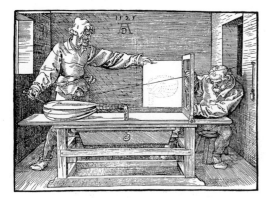

A woodcut from Dürer's *Introduction in the Art of Measurement with Compass and Ruler* shows an apparatus, apparently invented by Dürer, for translating three-dimensional objects into two-dimensional drawings. An artist is seated before his drawing, which is mounted on a hinged vertical frame atop a table that supports his subject, a lute. As his assistant swings the drawing aside, the artist sights along a string, the free end of which is held to a part of the lute. The string passes through the frame at a point that the artist fixes by crossing two threads, one horizontal and one vertical. The string is then released and the drawing swung back to the frame so that the artist can record on it the point marked by the intersection of the threads. The drawing is swung away again, the assistant moves the sight-string to another part of the lute, and the process is repeated. Gradually, the artist achieves a pinpointed outline of the lute in accurate perspective.

even cemeteries. Previous German artists had stuck to their workshops, but Dürer in this treatise—and indeed in all of his theoretical writings—moved from the studio to the company of his many-sided Renaissance contemporaries of the south, Leonardo and Michelangelo.

During the last months of his life Dürer concentrated his diminished energies on the four volumes of his *Treatise on Human Proportions,* two volumes of which he managed to complete before his death. He also had time to give Pirckheimer, who was to write the preface, some suggestions about points to stress, including an assurance that the book contained nothing "which is stolen from other sources."

In his opus Dürer tried laboriously to come to grips with the fundamental questions that had obsessed him since his first journey to Venice: What is the geometrical formula for proportion in art? How may the artist work as nature works? What general law can embrace all the particular varieties of human physique and character? In formulating his answers he discussed and diagrammed the proportions of various parts of the body according to a fixed scale; the construction of standard figures of men and women; the varying of proportions to produce different types; the proportional alteration of postures. Although he had set himself an impossible task, there is in this treatise much practical wisdom extracted from 40 years of working, searching and thinking. After Dürer's death Pirckheimer completed the book and saw it through the press. Its popularity was such that it went into 15 editions in seven different languages. Michelangelo considered it a waste of time, but it was still being used respectfully in the next century by Rubens, Rembrandt and Poussin.

Dürer planned one last instructional book in which he would hand down all his knowledge and experience as his legacy to those "able young men who love art more than silver and gold." But this *Food for Young Painters* was still only a fragment, a mass of notes, when he died suddenly on the sixth of April 1528.

"In Albrecht I have lost the best friend I ever had on earth," Pirckheimer wrote. Dürer was buried in the same cemetery of St. John that he had painted so precisely as an apprentice. Pirckheimer composed a funeral oration in Latin. Then, still grieving, he returned home and wrote a bitter letter accusing Agnes Dürer of having brought her husband to an early grave through her greedy and quarrelsome nature. Hans Baldung Grien, Dürer's most gifted and important pupil, begged a lock of his master's hair. Luther, by now two years married and with two children, wrote from Wittenberg:

"It is indeed the duty of pious men to mourn for Dürer . . . but Christ gave him a happy end and removed him from these troubled times, though there may be even more troubled ones ahead; so that he who deserved to witness only the best, at least was not compelled to witness the worst. May he rest in peace. Amen."

In that twilight period of the waning 15th Century, when the medieval order was breaking down and a new order was trying uncertainly to establish itself, out of the tensions of the era—and perhaps brought to fruition by them—Dürer emerged as the first modern artist north of the Alps. With him German art broke through the parochialism of the late

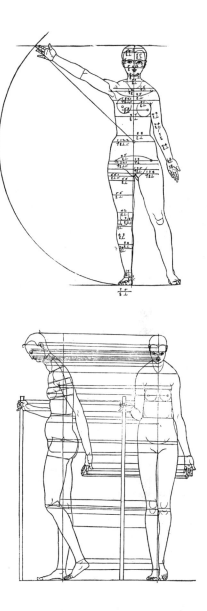

Sketches from Dürer's studies in proportion illustrate his search for scientific methods of drawing the human figure. At top he uses a circle centered on the navel to delimit the lengths of limbs; the rest of the body is marked off according to sets of fixed ratios (in this case the head is about one-eighth of the body). Above, Dürer's example shows how to transpose a figure from a profile view to a front view by using parallel reference lines.

Gothic to the universal. By his contemporaries he was recognized and acclaimed far more as a designer of woodcuts and an engraver than as a painter. The multiple reproductive possibilities of the printing press made him into an international figure. His *Feast of the Rose Garlands* might be the wonder of the season at Venice, but his *Apocalypse* and his *Passions* were household images from the Mediterranean to the Baltic. It may be argued whether *The Four Apostles* or Grünewald's Isenheim *Crucifixion* is the greater painting, whether Dürer's Nuremberg portraits or Holbein's more extensive London portraits are the more significant achievement. What is not arguable is the unsurpassed imaginative qualities of Dürer's chief woodcuts and engravings—and this judgment of his contemporaries has been sustained. In sheer quantity as well as quality he is unequaled, for he left a heritage of more than a thousand drawings—more than any other artist of the North except Rembrandt.

The court astronomer to Henry VIII, Niklas Kratzer, who had first met Dürer at Erasmus' house in the Netherlands, carried Dürer's prints to England. King Christian II distributed them in Scandinavia as presents. In their wide circulation across Europe they were as imitated as they were admired, reflected in painting and sculpture, in enamels and even Gobelin tapestries. Raphael kept Dürer's prints in his studio in Rome, and for his *Bearing of the Cross* borrowed the figure of Christ from the woodcut in *The Small Passion*. The most monumental of Dürer's later woodcuts, *The Trinity*—showing God the Father holding the broken body of Christ—was used by Tintoretto as a model for his *Lamentation*

Just as Dürer explored ideal human and animal proportions in two books, so he immersed himself in plans for an ideal military defense in a third work, his *Treatise on Fortifications*. This woodcut illustrates a method for protecting a city like Nuremberg against a besieging army. To the city's walls and towers he proposed adding a gigantic bastion fronted by a wide walled trench *(center, left)*. Artillery atop the bastion would shell enemy batteries, while soldiers in bunkers in the trench would engage any of the foe who scaled the outer wall.

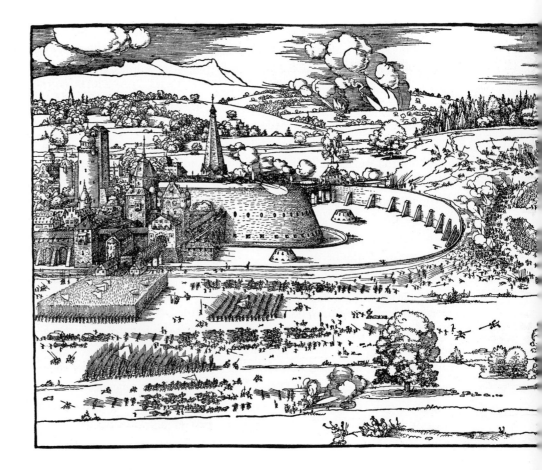

in the Doges' Palace in Venice, and its outlines and substance were absorbed by El Greco in his *Throne of Grace* in Madrid. Andrea del Sarto borrowed from the German master. The young Rembrandt copied the woodcut of *Christ Driving the Money-Lenders from the Temple* as carefully as the young Dürer had once copied Mantegna.

Dürer's genius embodied all the artistic aspirations of his time, and, from whatever altered perspective, his stature across the years has not diminished. He left no worthy successors, as he had hoped when he planned his theoretical works; and with the death of his younger contemporary, Holbein, the brief great flowering of German art ended.

With Goethe, Dürer remains the foremost embodiment of the German spirit, his art transcending nationalism to become the common property of mankind. Goethe's Faust—with his restless striving, his rejection of all boundaries, even those of space and time—is the symbol of Western man, no less so in the space age than when Goethe wrote. Yet Faust is merely the obverse of Dürer's Knight who goes resolutely on his way brooking no hindrance to his goal.

Pirckheimer composed the Latin epitaph marking Dürer's grave. It read: "Whate'er was mortal of Albrecht Dürer is interred beneath this mound." But Dürer in his *Treatise on Human Proportions* wrote his own epitaph in the language he had forged himself: "Occasionally God gives an artist the ability to learn and create something good; and no one like him can be found in his own time, or perhaps ever existed before him or will soon come after him."

Dürer's contemporaries and successors admired him extravagantly, but they went their own independent ways. This gave a lively diversity to 16th Century German art and produced such assorted talents as Albrecht Altdorfer, Lucas Cranach the Elder, Hans Baldung Grien and Hans Burgkmair. These, next to Dürer, Grünewald and Holbein, are regarded as the four best German painters of the era.

Altdorfer was addicted to landscapes and painted many lyrical scenes of his native region, the upper Danube Valley. Landscape painting also attracted Cranach, but he had the good luck to be made court painter to Frederick the Wise, also Dürer's patron, who recognized him as a first-rate portraitist. More important, Cranach later began turning out the slender, gauzily draped nudes that now instantly conjure up his name. Baldung Grien, an assistant of Dürer's, was also an accomplished painter of nudes, but his women lack the grace and mischievous sensuality of Cranach's.

Burgkmair delighted in decorative touches. His religious works—such as the dramatic altarpiece shown above and at right—abound in fruits, flowers and birds. Like Dürer, he esteemed the Italians, and absorbed their ideas on their home ground. Moving beyond the parochialism of Cranach and Baldung Grien, Burgkmair helped strengthen the ties that increasingly linked the art of North and South.

The German Flowering

The central panel of Burgkmair's triptych shows John the Evangelist on the Greek island of Patmos, in a swirl of leaves and birds such as Patmos probably never knew. The hare, partly hidden under the branch at lower right, may have been inspired by Dürer's watercolor (page 75).

Hans Burgkmair: *St. John Altarpiece*, 1518

164

Hans Baldung Grien: *Freiburg Altarpiece*, c. 1516

Hans Baldung Grien met Dürer in Alsace during Dürer's journeyman wanderings, and later became an assistant in his Nuremberg workshop. But Baldung Grien turned elsewhere for inspiration in his celebrated work, a triptych *(central panel above)* for Freiburg Cathedral's high altar. In intensity of color it recalls *The Isenheim Altarpiece,* but it is considerably lighter in emotional tone than Grünewald's stirring work.

Baldung Grien proved equally inventive in the allegory shown at right. Here he takes a recurrent German theme—the inevitable decay of the flesh—but transforms it with a cheerier note: by making the central female particularly robust, he optimistically reminds the viewer of life's ever-renewing cycle.

Hans Baldung Grien: *Three Ages of Woman and Death*, c. 1510

Cranach the Elder: *Johannes Cuspinian*, 1502-1503

Cranach the Elder: *Judith*, c. 1538-1539

Lucas Cranach, born in Kronach in Franconia in 1472, received his initial artistic training from his father. At the turn of the century he traveled to Austria, where he painted the rector of the University of Vienna, Johannes Cuspinian *(above, left)*. Cranach's early skill as a landscapist in the style of the Danube School is evident in the exquisite background of this work. In his later portraits he concentrated more attention on his subjects, often abandoning a scenic background entirely. Unrelieved black serves as the setting for his study *(above, right)* of an elegant court lady in the role of the Biblical heroine Judith, who cut off the head of the Assyrian Holofernes.

Cranach also painted many religious works, among them *The Holy Kinship (right)* a complex grouping of figures showing the Holy Family and various relatives dressed as 16th Century Germans. The somber figure at left may be Cranach himself.

Lucas Cranach the Elder: *The Holy Kinship*, 1510-1512

Cranach the Elder: *Judgment of Paris*, 1530

Cranach's crowning achievement was his nudes, and the Cranach nude is distinctive indeed. Long-legged, apple-breasted, with just a hint of a delicious little paunch, she is frankly seductive, her allure enhanced by a wisp of gauze, a fashionable hat or a rich necklace. These sinuously shaped sirens must have caused a sensation in their day, for the faces of many are believed to be recognizable portraits of the court ladies Cranach knew. Yet there was nothing scandalous per se in 16th Century Germany about the use of the nude. The upsurge of scholarly interest in classical antiquity, notably its statues, made nudity in art wholly acceptable. Even Erasmus' translation of the New Testament, published in 1519, featured naked women on its title page.

One of Cranach's masterpieces on a classical theme is his enchanting *Judgment of Paris (left).* There sits the Trojan Prince, transformed by Cranach into a stout German in full armor, getting a last bit of advice from Mercury, revamped into an elderly courtier. Paris seems dazed by the difficulty of his task —to choose the most beautiful of the goddesses arrayed before him. Which will it be: the maiden coyly clasping her foot, the one who holds back her arms to display her neat little bosom to best advantage, or the shy, hatted girl who just stands there? Will it be Juno, Minerva or Venus?

As the world knows, Paris picked Venus, and she rewarded him with the gift of another man's wife, Helen. But Helen's husband, the Greek King Menelaus, came after her, and the Trojan War resulted. In Cranach's canvas, this unhappy outcome merits no notice whatever; the artist has been content to capture a single delightful moment in mythological time.

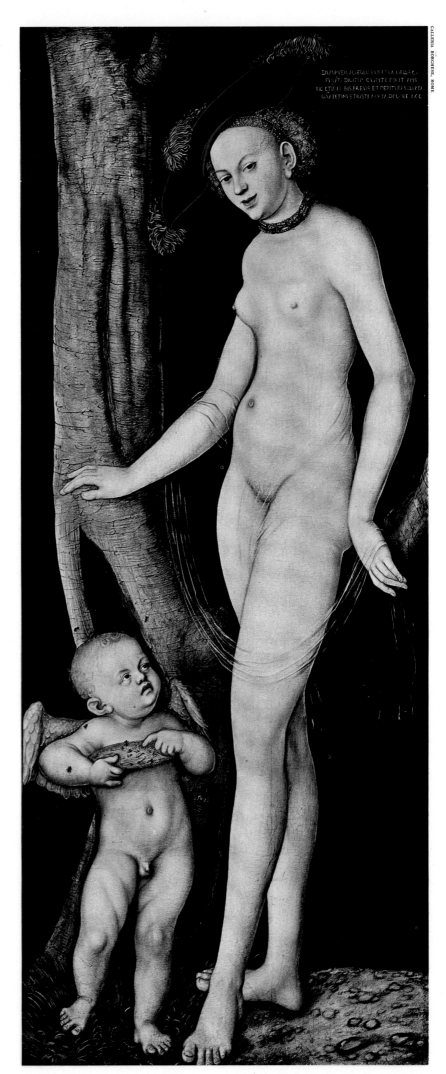

Cranach the Elder: *Venus and Cupid,* c. 1530-1531

Cranach worked diligently in the service of three Saxon princes, painting steadily for half a century. His output was enormous, but he never produced anything quite so unusual as his *Golden Age.* At first glimpse this seems to be a portrayal of a Germanic Eden with its fruit trees, its carpet of flowers, its pairs of gentle animals and, for good measure, a full dozen Adams and Eves cavorting in innocent nakedness.

It is only when the human figures are scrutinized more carefully that doubts arise about the meaning of this picture. These are real people; once again Cranach has been playing the game of putting men and women he knew into his allegorical canvases. And his audience must have been tempted to speculate about the real identity of that ever-so-wise young lady lying on the grass, patiently sizing up the worried young man next to her. What is their true relationship; who are they?

Compounding the confusion is the touch of irony that Cranach added. He has set his erotic scene inside a walled garden—a traditional Gothic symbol of the purity and innocence of the Virgin. His contemporaries may well have been shocked by this irreverent allusion to more orthodox paintings *(page 42).*

Perhaps Cranach is saying that Eden can be Eden only if it is not invaded by man, who will ultimately destroy it with the vanities and vices that he introduces. Or are we reading too much into the picture? Is this nothing more than the artist's vision of a happy time in the golden past when men and animals could play together in meadows ever green? One of the charms of Cranach is that he never quite explains himself.

Cranach the Elder: *The Golden Age*, c. 1530

Albrecht Altdorfer: *Forest Landscape with St. George Killing the Dragon,* 1510

Albrecht Altdorfer: *Battle of Alexander,* 1529

In contrast to Cranach, Albrecht Altdorfer never lost his passion for painting landscapes. He found an endless source of fascination in the broad sweep of his native countryside—the area around Regensburg in the upper Danube Valley—and was by far the greatest exponent of its regional style.

Altdorfer was involved with the total conception of a picture, subordinating details to express his feeling for the power and force of nature. In the small painting at top left, St. George and his dragon are almost obscured by their setting in a primordial forest; their forms melt into the trees, which are really more important than St. George himself.

In the later and much larger *Battle of Alexander (lower left, detail opposite),* commissioned by the Duke of Bavaria, the subject —Alexander's rout of Darius—is proclaimed on a plaque hanging fantastically above the turmoil of battle. Here again man is made secondary, this time to an overwhelming panorama of land, sea and sky. Although thousands of soldiers are locked in combat —Alexander and Darius are marked by banners to distinguish them from the horde—the human struggle takes place in an arena in which all nature is involved. Even the sun and the moon battle each other, brilliantly illuminating the scene in cosmic light.

Albrecht Altdorfer: *Battle of Alexander*, detail

CHRONOLOGY

Artists of Dürer's Era

	1400	1500	1600

GERMANY

HANS MULTSCHER c.1400–1467

STEPHAN LOCHNER c.1410–1451

MEISTER FRANCKE fl.1424–1435

LUCAS MOSER fl.1431–1440

CONRAD WITZ fl.1433–1447

MICHAEL WOLGEMUT 1434–1519

MICHAEL PACHER c.1435–1498

RUELAND FRUEAUF THE ELDER 1440/50–1507

VEIT STOSS 1447/48–1533

MARTIN SCHONGAUER c.1450–1491

HANS PLEYDENWURFF c.1451–1473

HANS HOLBEIN THE ELDER 1460–1524

BERNARD STRIGEL 1460/61–1528

GRÜNEWALD c.1470–1528

ALBRECHT DÜRER 1471–1528

LUCAS CRANACH THE ELDER 1472–1553

HANS BURGKMAIR 1473–1531

JÖRG BREU c.1475–1537

HOUSEBOOK MASTER fl.1480–1490

HANS SUESS VON KULMBACH 1480–1522

ALBRECHT ALTDORFER c.1480–1538

HANS SCHÄUFELEIN 1480/85–1538/40

LEONHARD BECK c.1480–1542

HANS BALDUNG GRIEN 1480–1545

WOLF TRAUT 1485–1520

HANNS DÜRER 1490–c.1534

HANS SPRINGINKLEE 1490/95–c.1540

WOLF HUBER c.1490–1553

BARTHEL BRUYN 1492/93–1555

HANS HOLBEIN THE YOUNGER 1497–1543

GEORG PENCZ 1500–1550

SEBALD BEHAM 1500–1550

BARTHEL BEHAM 1502–1540

FRANCE

ENGUERRAND QUARTON c.1410–1461

JEAN FOUQUET c.1420–1481

SIMON MARMION 1420/25–1489

THE MASTER OF KING RENÉ D'ANJOU fl.1445–1470

NICOLAS FROMENT fl.1450–1490

MAÎTRE DE MOULINS fl.1480

JEAN CLOUET 1485–1541

JEAN DUVET 1485–c.1561

FRANÇOIS CLOUET c.1510–1572

	1400	1500	1600

FLANDERS

ROBERT CAMPIN 1375–1444

JAN VAN EYCK c.1390–1441

ROGIER VAN DER WEYDEN c.1399–1464

PETRUS CHRISTUS c.1410–1472

DIRCK BOUTS c.1420–1475

HANS MEMLING c.1430–1494

HUGO VAN DER GOES c.1440–1482

HIERONYMUS BOSCH c.1450–1516

GERARD DAVID c.1450–1523

GEERTGEN TOT SINT JANS 1460/65–1490/95

QUENTIN MASSYS c.1466–1530

MABUSE (JAN GOSSAERT) c.1470–1533

JOACHIM PATINIER c.1475–1524

JOOS VAN CLEVE 1485–1540/41

BERNARD VAN ORLEY c.1488–1541

LUCAS VAN LEYDEN 1494–1533

JAN VAN SCOREL 1495–1562

PIETER BRUEGEL THE ELDER 1525–1569

ITALY

FRA FILIPPO LIPPI 1406–1469

PIERO DELLA FRANCESCA c.1416–1492

GENTILE BELLINI c.1429–1507

ANTONELLO DA MESSINA c.1430–1479

GIOVANNI BELLINI c.1430–1516

ANTONIO POLLAIUOLO c.1431–1498

ANDREA MANTEGNA 1431–1506

JACOPO DE' BARBARI 1440/50–1516

LUCA SIGNORELLI c.1441–1523

SANDRO BOTTICELLI c.1444–1510

PIETRO PERUGINO c.1445–1523

DOMENICO GHIRLANDAIO 1449–1494

LEONARDO DA VINCI 1452–1519

VITTORE CARPACCIO c.1455–1526

FRA BARTOLOMMEO 1472–1517

MICHELANGELO 1475–1564

GIORGIONE c.1478–1510

RAPHAEL 1483–1520

ANDREA DEL SARTO 1486–1531

TITIAN c.1487–1576

CORREGGIO 1494–1534

PONTORMO c.1494–1557

FRANCESCO PARMIGIANINO 1503–1540

JACOPO TINTORETTO 1518–1594

	1400	1500	1600

Dürer's predecessors, contemporaries and successors are grouped here in chronological order according to country. The bands correspond to the life-spans of the artists or, where this information is unknown, to the approximate periods when they flourished (indicated by the abbreviation "fl.").

Bibliography   * Paperback.

DÜRER—LIFE AND WORKS

Anzelewski, Fedja, *Dürer and His Time.** Smithsonian Publication. An exhibition catalogue.

Conway, William Martin (editor), *The Writings of Albrecht Dürer*. Philosophical Library, Inc., 1958.

Grote, Ludwig, *Dürer*. Translated by Helga Harrison. Editions d'Art Albert Skira, Geneva, 1965.

Homolka, Jaromir, *The Feast of the Rose Garlands*. Spring Books, London, 1961.

Knappe, Karl-Adolf, *Dürer, the Complete Engravings, Etchings and Woodcuts*. Harry N. Abrams, Inc., 1965.

Kurth, Willi (editor), *The Complete Woodcuts of Albrecht Dürer.** Dover Publications, 1961.

Levey, Michael, *Dürer*. W. W. Norton Company, 1964.

Musper, A. T., *Dürer*. Translated by Robert Erich Wolf. Harry N. Abrams, Inc., 1966.

Panofsky, Erwin, *The Life and Art of Albrecht Dürer*, 2 vols. Princeton University Press, 1943. Rev. ed. The definitive study. Volume Two is a complete listing and concordance of all Dürer's works.

Schilling, Edmund, *Albrecht Dürer, Drawings and Water Colors*. Wasserman AG, Basel, 1949.

Steck, Max, *Dürer and his world*. Translated by J. Maxwell Brownjohn. The Viking Press, 1964.

Waetzoldt, Wilhelm, *Dürer and His Times*. Translated by R. H. Boothroyd. Phaidon Publishers, Inc., London, 1950.

Winkler, Friedrich, *Die Zeichnungen Albrecht Dürers*, 4 vols. Deutscher Verein Für Kunstwissenschaft, Berlin, 1936-1939. The complete drawings with introduction and notes in German.

ART-HISTORICAL BACKGROUND

Benesch, Otto:
The Art of the Renaissance in Northern Europe. Archon Books, 1964.
German Painting. Translated by H.S.B. Harrison. Editions d'Art Albert Skira, Geneva, 1966.

Gombrich, Ernst, *The Story of Art.** Phaidon Publishers, Inc., London, 1966.

Janson, H. W., *History of Art*. Harry N. Abrams, Inc., 1962.

Panofsky, Erwin, *Early Netherlandish Painting*. Harvard University Press, 1964.

Stange, Alfred:
Deutsche Malerei der Gotik, 11 vols. Deutscher Kunstverlag, Munich & Berlin, 1934-1961.
German Painting, XIV-XVI Centuries. Hyperion Press, London, 1950.

Venturi, Lionello, *The Sixteenth Century*. Translated by Stuart Gilbert. Editions d'Art Albert Skira, Geneva, 1956.

Wölfflin, Heinrich, *The Sense of Form in Art*. Chelsea Publishing Company, 1958. (First edition: Munich, 1931.)

OTHER GERMAN ARTISTS

Chamberlain, Arthur B., *Hans Holbein the Younger*. Dodd, Mead & Company, 1913.

Conway, William Martin, "Dürer and the Housebook Master," *The Burlington Magazine*, Vol. XVIII, 1910/11, pp. 317-324.

Descargues, Pierre, *Cranach*. Harry N. Abrams, Inc., 1961.

Ganz, Paul, *The Paintings of Hans Holbein*. Phaidon Publishers, Inc., London, 1950.

Geisberg, Max, *Martin Schongauer*. Knoedler & Company, 1928.

Huysmans, J. K., *Grünewald—the Paintings*. Phaidon Publishers, Inc., London, 1958.

Ivins, W. M. Jr., "Martin Schongauer," *Arts*, Vol. XIII, 1922, pp. 169-171.

Lehrs, Max, *The Master of the Amsterdam Cabinet*. International Chalcographical Society, Paris.

Pevsner, Nikolaus and Michael Meier, *Grünewald*. Harry N. Abrams, Inc., 1958.

Ruhmer, Eberhard, *Cranach*. Translated by Joan Spencer. Phaidon Publishers, Inc., London, 1963.

Schmid, H. A., *Hans Holbein der Jüngere. Sein Aufsteig zur Meisterschaft und sein englischer Stil*, 3 vols. Holbein Verlag, Basel, 1948.

Stange, Alfred, *Der Hausbuchmeister*. Editions P. H. Heitz, Baden-Baden & Strasbourg, 1958.

CULTURAL AND HISTORICAL BACKGROUND

Barraclough, Geoffrey, *The Origins of Modern Germany*. Basil Blackwell, Oxford, 1947.

Bryce, James, *The Holy Roman Empire*. The Macmillan Company, 1904.

Dickens, A. G., *Reformation and Society in Sixteenth-Century Europe*. Harcourt, Brace & World, 1966.

Ferguson, Wallace K., *Europe in Transition*. Houghton Mifflin, 1962.

Fisher, H.A.L., *A History of Europe*. Houghton Mifflin, 1935.

Gilmore, Myron P., *The World of Humanism*. Harper & Brothers, 1952.

Headlam, Cecil, *The Story of Nuremberg*. J. M. Dent & Company, London, 1899.

Holborn, Hajo, *A History of Modern Germany: The Reformation*. Alfred A. Knopf, 1961.

Huizinga, Johan, *The Waning of the Middle Ages.** Anchor Books, 1954.

Janssen, Johannes, *History of the German People at the Close of the Middle Ages*, 17 vols. Translated by M. A. Mitchell and A. M. Christie. Kegan Paul, Trench, Trubner & Co., Ltd., London, 1905-1925.

Lucas, H., *Renaissance and Reformation*. Harper & Brothers, 1934.

Stubbs, William, *Germany in the Later Middle Ages*. Longmans, Green & Company, 1908.

Taylor, H. O., *Thought and Expression in the Sixteenth Century*, 2 vols. The Macmillan Company, 1920.

Thompson, S. Harrison. *Europe in Renaissance and Reformation*. Harcourt, Brace & World, 1963.

Valentin, Veit. *The German People*. Alfred A. Knopf, 1946.

Zu Loewenstein, Hubertus, *The Germans in History*. Columbia University Press, 1945.

PRINTING AND THE GRAPHIC ARTS

Hind, Arthur M.:
*A History of Engraving and Etching.** Dover Publications, Inc., 1963. (First edition: Houghton Mifflin, 1923.)
An Introduction to a History of the Woodcut, 2 vols.* Dover Publications, Inc., 1963. (First edition: Houghton Mifflin, 1935.)

Ivins, William M., Jr., *How Prints Look.** Beacon Press, 1958.

Steinberg, S. H., *Five Hundred Years of Printing.** Penguin Books, Harmondsworth, Middlesex, 1961.

Acknowledgments

The editors are particularly indebted to Dr. Carol Krinsky, Assistant Professor at Washington Square College of New York University, for her valuable guidance on many parts of this book. She is the author of numerous scholarly articles on Late Medieval and Early Renaissance art.

For their generous cooperation, the editors also wish to thank the following individuals and institutions: Mrs. Renate Antonio, Graphische Sammlung Albertina, Vienna; Luisa Becherucci, Director, Galleria degli Uffizi, Florence; Mrs. A. E. van Beuningen-Charlouis, Rotterdam; Museum Boymans van Beuningen, Rotterdam; The Brooklyn Museum, New York; Lieselotte Camp, Alte Pinakothek, Munich; Castle Museum, Darmstadt; Charles Fellmann, Régisseur du Musée Unterlinden, Colmar; The Fogg Art Museum, Cambridge, Massachusetts; Ernst Hofmann, Darm-stadt; David Johnson, Prints Division, New York Public Library; Wilhelm Köhler, Gemaeldegalerie Staatliche Museen zu Berlin; Walter Koschatzky, Director, Graphische Sammlung Albertina, Vienna; Maria José de Mendoça, Curator, Museu Nacional de Arte Antiga, Lisbon; The Metropolitan Museum of Art, New York; Abel de Moura, Curator, Museu Nacional, Lisbon; Hans Heinrich Richter, Deutsche Fotothek, Dresden; Prentenkabinet Rijksmuseum, Amsterdam; Elizabeth Roth, Prints Division, New York Public Library; Pastor Otto Michael Schmitt, Freiburg Cathedral; Halldor Soehner, General Director, Bayrische Staatsgemaeldesammlung, Munich; Stephan Waetzholdt, General Director, and Staff, Staatliche Museen, Berlin; Erich Steingraber, Director, Germanisches Nationalmuseum, Nuremberg; Fritz Zink, Head of Print Room, Germanisches Nationalmuseum, Nuremberg.

Picture Credits

The sources for the illustrations in this book are shown below. Credits for pictures from left to right are separated by commas, from top to bottom by dashes.

Albrecht Dürer: *Self Portrait,* 1498. A detail of the painting in color appears on the slipcase.

Index

The text for this book was set in photocomposed Bembo. First cut in Europe in 1930, Bembo is named for the Italian humanist Pietro Bembo (1470-1547), an arbiter of literary taste. While it has some resemblance to letters designed in 1470 by Nicholas Jenson, it is largely based on characters cut by Francesco Griffo around 1490.

✗✗✗✗✗

Printed in U.S.A.